BEER BY
DESIGN

The Art of Good Beer Branding

PETE BROWN
with Liz Vater

CAMRA
BOOKS

Published by the Campaign for Real Ale Ltd
230 Hatfield Road, St Albans, Hertfordshire AL1 4LW
www.camra.org.uk/books

© Campaign for Real Ale Ltd. 2020
First published 2020
Reprinted 2021

ISBN 978-1-85249-368-4

A CIP catalogue record for this book is available from the British Library

Printed in the UK by CPI Antony Rowe, Chippenham, Wiltshire.

Managing Editor: Alan Murphy
Design/typography: Dale Tomlinson
Sales & Marketing: Toby Langdon

Contents

The authors

Pete Brown is an author, journalist, broadcaster and consultant specialising in food and drink, especially the fun parts like beer, pubs, cider, and fish and chips. Across eleven books, his broad, fresh approach takes in social history, cultural commentary, travel writing, personal discovery and natural history, and his words are always delivered with the warmth and wit you'd expect from a great night down the pub. He was named British Beer Writer of the Year in 2009, 2012 and 2016, has won three Fortnum & Mason Food and Drink Awards, and has been shortlisted twice for the André Simon Awards. Pete is Chair of the British Guild of Beer Writers.

Liz Vater worked with some of the world's leading design and advertising agencies for over 20 years, before setting up the Stoke Newington Literary Festival in 2010. During lockdown, she accidentally became an award-winning publisher (of Pete's book *Craft: An Argument*). Deciding that resistance was futile, she became a fully fledged beer fan when she married Pete.

Acknowledgements

Pete would like to thank Silas Amos, Malcolm Garrett, Neil Gower, Sarah Hyndman, Alec Tear, and all the brewers and designers who made this book possible. Thank you to Dusty Miller for the original inspiration, to Alan Murphy for asking, 'Have you got an idea for a book that you can turn around quickly without leaving your home?' at the start of Covid-19 lockdown, and to Dale Tomlinson for making this book look as beautiful as it needed to.

Liz would like to thank the hundreds of brewery workers, designers, photographers, artists and illustrators who responded so enthusiast-ically to provide the visual content of this book. Their energy and positivity, and the stories they were keen to tell, made the mammoth task of researching this book a joyful and inspiring experience.

'we try harder'

Introduction

Does anyone still say 'Don't judge a book by its cover?'
Because everyone does that, really, and I'm not sure
why we were ever advised not to. How else do you get
from walking into a shop that stocks 45,000 titles, to
browsing a handful, picking a few up, and hopefully taking
one or two of them to the till? Book covers are carefully
designed to convey the type of book contained within,
to follow category norms that say 'This is a thriller', or
'This is a romance'. If you're reading this after being attracted
to the cover in a bookshop and picking it up, thank you.
I guess some aspect of the cover design worked here too.

I've never heard anyone say 'Don't judge a record by
its sleeve'. I have records in my collection that I bought
entirely because of the sleeve design, having never heard
the songs contained within. There were cues and clues
in the artwork, or the lettering. Maybe I recognised the
designer and knew the kinds of bands they worked with?
Or maybe I just intuited the style of music because
I already have loads of records in a genre I love and
which have similar typefaces or artwork.

Think about the last time you were in a shop or supermarket, and you picked up a brand you'd neither seen nor
heard of before. What was it that stood out? What was
it that suggested – probably in a fraction of a second –
that this might be something that was right for you?

It's been estimated that we see anywhere from 4,000 to 10,000 commercial messages every day. Or rather, we're *exposed* to that many; our brains aren't capable of processing that much visual information at a conscious, cognitive level. Much of what we see communicates information at a level below conscious awareness, but we're also becoming increasingly adept at filtering out the messages that don't matter to us, in the same way you can listen to a babble of conversation and noise in a crowded place and pick out the voice of your partner or child.

A typical supermarket carries around 35,000 different product lines. If we were to examine them all, we'd never finish a shop. The number of choices we face in anything we buy is increasing exponentially. It gets harder and harder for a brand to be noticed, so brands turn to newer and more sophisticated techniques in an attempt to cut through the noise. Or at least, the smart brands do. Many more just shout ever more loudly in our faces. Advertising bombards us from

With thousands of brands shouting at us, we use subliminal visual cues to narrow down our choices.

every angle: no longer just billboards, TV and radio, but also flashing up on every page we browse on the internet, in our text messages, on the backs of the seats in front of us on planes and trains, in toilet cubicles and on hand driers. Pretty much any public space is now colonised by commercial messages, and we're receiving a steady stream of them all the time we're watching any kind of screen.

Many of us eventually suffer from 'choice fatigue'. Have you ever felt a sense of rising panic when looking at a menu while a server hovers above you, or while standing at the bar as the barperson stares at you and you can feel the eyes of people behind you boring into the back of your skull? It may only last for a moment, but when it happens, it feels like genuine distress. We feel overwhelmed by the experience, and, in a panic, we often default to what we know, reassuring ourselves that the modern, social media-driven phenomenon of FOMO (fear of missing out) is countered by the fact that in all this confusion, we've made a safe choice. Knowing that we're probably going to do this only makes new brands trying to attract our attention shout even louder, as the old ones try to reassure us that they're as good now as they've always been.

This phenomenon of overwhelming choice is particularly rife in the beer market. The number of breweries in Britain rose from 500 at the millennium to over 2,500 in 2018. The vast majority of these breweries brew ranges of beer rather than just one product, with core ranges complemented by seasonals, special editions and collaborations. Throw in beers imported from other countries, and at any given time there are more than 10,000 different beers on sale. The average pub now sells between fifteen and twenty-two different beers on the bar, compared with four or five twenty years ago. In the off-trade, a quick search for 'Beer' on tesco.com returns 225 items.

Over the same period as this explosion of choice, total beer sales in the UK fell from 57 million hectolitres to 45 million hectolitres. This means we now have five times as many brewers chasing four-fifths of the demand compared to twenty years ago. If you want to make it as a brewer, brewing good beer is vital of course. But even if you have the best beer in the world, how do you get people to notice it and pick it up, or ask for it at the bar?

In this crazily competitive environment, how a beer looks has never been more important. And that's why trends in beer branding have never moved faster. Beer was, for a long time, very conservative in how it looked; big on history and continuity. I was surprised while researching this book how recently it was that colourful, attractive fonts and labels came to be standard.

The proverb 'Don't judge a book by its cover' means 'never make a judgement about anything based on how it first appears'. It can be used both positively and negatively: that massive guy over there with the biker badges, leather, tats and furious expression looks scary, but when you talk to him he's the sweetest guy you've ever met. But when it's applied more literally in a commercial sense, we often mean 'Don't be taken in by fancy packaging – that's no guarantee the product will be any good.'

It's very common among beer fans – be they real ale aficionados, craft beer cognoscenti, or both – to protest strongly that they're not influenced by marketing: all that matters is the beer itself. Marketing is what Big Beer does, they argue, attracting undiscerning sheeple who drink tasteless, bland beers that differ from each other only by what's on the can or bottle.

Unless you're visually impaired to a degree that you can't see the branding, this denial is almost certainly not true. Every draught beer needs a pump clip or lens; every bottle or can needs a label or some identifying mark printed onto it. As soon as a brewer starts thinking about what goes into this small space, they're thinking about marketing-led design. As soon as a drinker looks at what ends up there, they are being influenced – knowingly or not – by that design. Consciously or not, they are looking for signs, hints and clues as to whether the beer they are looking at is one they will like.

Marketing is a dirty word that gets a bad rap. As with any other medium of communication, there's good and bad

THE WESTMINSTER ARMS (TEL. WESTMINSTER 365)

FINEST TABLE BEER & ALE ∙ EAST INDIA PALE ALE A.K. ∙ OATMEAL STOUT

Lost in the forest: pub bar tops have grown densely crowded over the last twenty years.

within it. Marketing cynics will point to its capacity to deceive, and it's true there are countless examples of marketing messages that mislead, even if the occurrence of outright lies is much lower than many people think. It's common for a brand to attempt to look 'premium' compared to others. But there would be little point in a real ale packaging itself to look like a can of mainstream lager, or vice-versa: the beer would fail to appeal to the target audience and most likely disappoint people who chose the beer under false impressions.

I worked in marketing before I became a writer, and studied for a degree in marketing before that. At its best, when it's done well, marketing can be very democratic: competing brands each make their case to the consumer, and the consumer has the final choice over which one to buy. Any marketer is looking to put the best case they can, but I always subscribed to a strand of marketing that one guru termed 'The truth, well told'. Sure, hire professionals to help you tell your story as best you possibly can, but I, and many like me, always operated on the principle of finding a group of people who might be interested in what you have to say, listening to what they wanted, and tailoring the message, and often the product, to meet their needs better than any of our competitors could. I still see nothing at all wrong with marketing in those terms. I quit the career after working with one client too many who saw marketing in a different way.

While it's easy to paint a negative picture of consumers being bombarded with commercial messages, like I just did, there's a lot of enjoyment to be had from celebrating the work of those who do it best.

In 2014 some colleagues and I founded the Beer and Cider Marketing Awards. Our aim was to make the competition relevant to brewers or cider makers of any size. We recruited judges from breweries, design agencies, pubs and beer communication. Ten years earlier, the winners of each category would have been the brewers with the biggest budgets and the best ad agencies, but by the mid-2010s things had become much more democratic: you can run a campaign on Twitter or Facebook for free. If you come up with a great PR idea that doesn't require a budget, you can still make it go viral. And if you've got a mate who went to design college, or you know a local artist, you can swap some beer in return for them making your range look way cooler and more contemporary than conservative big beer brands that can't risk too much change because of their size. The packaging design category in our awards would sometimes receive almost as many more entries as the other twelve categories combined, flooding in from brewers of all sizes, and we often ended up with designs that had spent years being developed by a top agency, painstakingly researched at every stage, competing with something that started off as a doodle on a beer mat and made it onto the side of a can a few weeks later.

While there is no shortage of beer brands that just want to shout in your face louder and louder, there are also brands that want to entertain, intrigue and make you smile. Good packaging doesn't just say, 'Here I am, look at me!' It can also tell a story about the brand. In ways we sometimes process

so quickly we're not aware of it, good design can excite us,
reassure us, intrigue us or tickle us. And there's more good
design around in beer than ever before.

In the next chapter, we'll explore the history of beer brand
design, from the UK's first ever trade mark to the craft beer
revolution that has made beer unrivalled by any other product
category in the creativity and diversity of its design.

We'll then lift the lid on how design works, some of the
tricks it plays and how it manages to encode a lot of information that we process intuitively, often without even noticing.
We'll explain how the design industry refined their techniques,
and how this led to the conventions and clichés that make
beer look the way it does.

Then, we break design down into its component parts:
typography, names and logos, visual designs, bottle shapes,
bottle closures, secondary packaging and other frills, showing
page after page of the most gorgeous, striking and effective
design we've found on sale in the UK.

It would be easy to show plenty of horror stories as well. If you want to see how atrocious beer design can be, the appalling cartoons, the sexist and offensive names, awful puns and amateurish scribbles, check out my mate Jeff Pickthall's blog, 'Pump Clip Parade' (www.pumpclipparade.co.uk). This stuff should be called out and held to account, and Jeff does it brilliantly. But we decided that this book would focus solely on good work; that it should be something beer fans – and connoisseurs of great design – can pick up and flick through, and appreciate as they would an art book.

It is, of course, best appreciated with a beer in hand. We can by no means guarantee that every beer featured in these pages tastes like angels dancing on your tongue. We've made no judgement on the quality of the beer, whether the brewer making it is real ale, craft or macro, good or bad at what they brew. Uniquely in the UK at the time of writing, this book celebrates the brewer's art outside the can, bottle, glass or beer font, rather than what's inside. Having said that, in collecting the artwork for this book, we've learned that many talented brewers are completists, looking for design that reflects the quality and character of their beer, and is executed to the same high standards. They are the ones hoping you will judge the book by its cover.

The revolution in the packaging design of beer mirrors that in the brewing of beer itself.

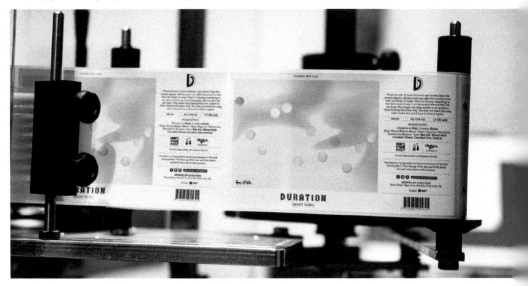

‘the real thing’

1

A Quick History of Beer Branding

The origin and definition of branding

Dictionaries carry two main definitions of the word 'brand'. One is 'An identifying mark burned on livestock or (especially in former times) criminals or slaves with a branding iron'. The word 'brand' dates back to the Norse word *brandr*, which means 'to burn'. The second is 'A type of product manufactured by a particular company under a particular name'.

The first definition gave birth to the second. A brand at its most basic is an identifying mark that makes it clear who owns, or who made, the thing being branded. Cattle brands are simple shapes, lines or letters. Early commercial brands weren't much more complicated, and for a population that was largely illiterate, a brand had to be visually clear and simple: an X, two XXs or even XXXX; a triangle or a (double) diamond.

Branding on cattle was introduced by the Ancient Egyptians, and dates back to at least 2700BCE. If someone attempted to steal cattle, anyone could see from the brand who its rightful owner was. In the Middle Ages, craftsmen would leave a distinctive mark on their work so customers could see who had made it; stylised signatures on paintings work in a similar way, as marks of authenticity. In 1266 the first trade mark legislation was passed, requiring bakers to use a distinctive mark on all the bread they sold.

Commercial branding is still about stopping someone from pretending property belongs to someone it doesn't, but in quite a different way from stealing cattle. Instead of stealing the product from its rightful owner, branding prevents an unscrupulous producer from passing off their product as someone else's. If you preferred baker A's bread to baker B's, you would look for their distinguishing mark. If baker B got jealous and wanted to attract your custom by nefarious means, they might try to copy baker A's mark and pass their bread off as their own. Manufacturers of branded goods responded by making their brands harder to copy, and also by legal action. Brands and forgeries were an increasing source of income to the legal profession over the nineteenth century. In 1862 the Merchandise Marks Act made it a criminal offence for baker B to copy baker A's distinguishing mark 'with intent to defraud or to enable another to defraud'. In 1875 the Trade Marks Registration Act allowed formal registration of trade marks at the UK Patent Office for the first time. Registration was considered to be hard evidence of ownership of any registered trade mark, defined as 'a device, or mark, or name of an individual or firm printed in some particular and distinctive manner; or a written signature or copy of a written signature of an individual or firm; or a distinctive label or ticket'. In addition, any word or name that was in use as a trade mark before the act was passed was entitled to registration, whether or not it fulfilled these criteria. The first such registered trade mark, on the day the legislation came into effect, was Bass Ale, on 1st January 1876. In 1883 the Patents and Trade Marks Act substantially revised trade mark law, reducing the cost of application, and included the facility to register 'fancy words not in common use' and 'brands' as new marks for the first time.

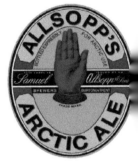

Beers destined for travel, particularly export, needed to be clearly branded as a guarantee of authenticity. Simple devices such as the Allsopp's red hand were instantly recognisable. Often, beers would be shipped in bulk and bottled when they reached their destination. Bottling the beer in good condition was a skill in its own right, to the extent that people would choose to buy certain bottlers as well as brewers. Nineteenth-century beer labels, therefore, often left space for the bottler to add their own branding, in a foretaste of the modern trend for collaboration beers.

BASS

The story of the UK's first trade mark

The problem with unscrupulous brewers passing off their own beers as those of far superior brewers was a common problem in the mid-nineteenth century, but for famous brands such as Bass, Allsopp and Guinness, the headache was particularly acute.

These beers had a reputation for keeping well and so were particularly focused on export. At a time when many brewers were acquiring pubs and tying them to sell only their own beers, Bass and others pioneered the use of bottles which were sold mainly through independent agents and merchants, or even sent to other countries to be bottled on arrival, making it far harder to keep track of any fakes.

From at least the 1850s Bass marked its barrels with triangles: red, white and blue, depending on whether it was brewed at the Old Brewery, the Middle Brewery or the New Brewery in Burton-on-Trent. All bottles of Bass Pale Ale carried the red triangle, a simple, iconic design that quickly became world famous.

'It is no extravagant assertion to say that throughout the world there is no name more familiar than that of Bass,' reads a passage in *Fortunes Made in Business*, a book written by 'Various Authors' and published in 1884. 'There is no geometrical figure so well known as the vermilion triangle which is the trademark on his [Mr Bass's] bottles. It is as familiar to the eye as Her Majesty's visage on the postage stamps.'

It took a great deal of skill and attention to detail to make Bass so famous and highly regarded. It was far easier to make inferior beer and sell it pretending it was Bass, copying the famous label which was so recognisable. In 1862 the brewery's London manager, Thomas Cooper Coxon, told a parliamentary hearing that he had collected fake Bass labels from Bremen, Paris, Dublin, Glasgow and Liverpool.

Part of the problem was that the simple marque was ridiculously easy to copy. Bass began making their full label more ornate, using Staffordshire knots around the edge, and giving it a kind of watermark effect. This didn't stop the use of fakes, but it did make them easier to spot.

Bass and other brewers such as Allsopp's lobbied persistently through the 1860s and early 1870s for legal protection of their logos, and were successful in suing people who passed off their own beers as the real thing. Finally, in 1875, parliament passed the Trade Marks Act to give legal protection to commercial marks. The Act came into force on

1st January 1876. The famous but uncorroborated story is that a clerk from Bass camped out on the steps of the new trade mark office the night before it opened so he could be sure of making Bass the UK's first ever trade mark.

It's not *quite* true to say that the famous red triangle was the UK's first trade mark though. Kicking off a theme that has become a regular headache in the history of trade marks, the first Trade Mark Act didn't allow colour specifically to be registered as something that was ownable. All registered marks initially appeared in black and white. Although it was understood that the triangle was usually red when used, the *red* triangle wasn't registered by Bass until 1885, after the supplementary 1883 Patents and Trade Marks Act broadened the scope of what could be registered.

The evolution of beer packaging

Once, beer was sold directly and consumed quickly.
The storage was done at the brewery, in big oak vats,
and once it was on sale, it was expected to be drunk.

Glass bottles have been around since the 1600s, but until
the mid-nineteenth century glass was expensive. Beer was
mostly carried in wood or ceramics and drunk from ceramic,
wood or pewter tankards. Glass was taxed at up to 300%
of its value, until 1845, when Sir Robert Peel abolished the
glass tax to help the spread of windows and natural light.

By the 1880s there were several large commercial glass
manufacturing plants, and the storage and sale of food and
drink in glass bottles and jars became increasingly common.
There wasn't as much need for this in beer as there was with
some other products, because it was still mostly drunk in pubs,
many belonging to the breweries that brewed the beer. But
brewers like Bass, Allsopp's and Guinness favoured a broader
retail approach with significant degree of export rather
than focusing on buying pubs to tie their route to market.

Luxuriating in the new affordability of glass, early beer
bottles were thick, with the brand name and logo heavily
embossed onto the surface.

In the late nineteenth century the demand for beer
peaked. The brewing industry began to consolidate, with
a process of mergers and acquisitions that saw the total
number of brewers shrink, as those that remained competed
across ever-larger territories instead of just servicing their
local communities. Competition became more intense.
Brewers rushed to tie pubs and create estates that only
sold their own beers. Those that sold beer outside pubs
had to give their bottles greater stand-out.

Non-standardised bottle shapes with
glass and embossed naming used to be
necessity before labelling. If they are
today, they symbolise superior quality

Printed paper labels had been around since the eighteenth century. They would have been one colour and hand-printed on wooden presses. Then, in 1796, German actor and playwright Alois Senefelder invented the lithography press, which printed labels in mass quantities. This was great if you were handing out flyers to promote a play, but if you wanted to affix them to a bottle, they still had to be hand-glued. Adhesives improved, and in 1845 the first postage stamps demonstrated how much easier it was to affix a paper label to something. In the 1850s various innovations in lithograph printing made rich, multi-coloured labels a possibility. Brewers took full advantage of the new technologies, particularly for export. As well as the name of the brewer and the beer, bright, distinguishing marks were now easy to reproduce, and labels could carry much more information. When beers were exported, they often travelled in barrels, with empty bottles sent along for bottling at the destination. Bottling was a skill in its own right, and beer labels would often leave space for the bottler to add their own name and trade mark, arguably the precursor to modern craft collaboration-branded beers.

Bottles were originally sealed with corks. If the contents were bottle conditioned, with live yeast creating a natural carbonation, these corks would be held in place by a wire cage to prevent the pressure from shooting them out. For beers designed for ageing, this would then be covered with a wax seal to prevent oxygen getting in or pressurised carbon dioxide from getting out. Screw caps developed as a more practical alternative, the screw performing the function of cork and wire cage in one. The only problem for brewers was that screws and corks could be replaced and reused, so it became common practice to place an additional paper seal over the top of the cork or screw, with words along the lines of 'Make sure this seal is unbroken' ensuring that no one had adulterated the beer or topped it up with something else. The invention of the crown cap in 1892 by William Painter finally provided a one-time seal that guaranteed quality but couldn't be reused for nefarious purposes.

The increasing sophistication of branding

While it looked sophisticated at the time compared to what had gone before, beer design remained fairly simple by modern standards until the 1930s, when the growing popularity of off-sales for drinking at home made bottles more important. This was the period when homes began their transformation from rude hovels where we slept and ate into spaces where we actually chose to spend time, with light, heat, ovens and radio, and mass-produced furniture becoming more affordable. Brewers who were seeing pubs struggle under new licensing laws and new leisure alternatives began suggesting that we might pick up a case of beer for when we kicked off our shoes and relaxed, or to accompany the evening meal.

They were helped by two major innovations. In 1935 American entrepreneur R. Stanton Avery invented the self-adhesive label, or 'sticker'. Now, everything from postage stamps, address labels and bottle labels to collectable stickers and temporary badges could be licked and stuck, or peeled from a backing strip and applied to surfaces including paper, metal, glass and plastic.

That same year, the first commercial beer can was launched. The American Can Company had developed beer cans as early as 1931 to take advantage of the anticipated demise of prohibition. Cans were lighter, easier to stack, and more efficient than glass in withstanding the pressure of their carbonated contents. There was just one problem: cans needed a lining that would prevent the metal from tainting the flavour of the beer. Brewers who acquired the technology were hesitant to launch cans for fear of damaging their reputation so soon after regaining the legal right to sell beer. The first to take the plunge was Krueger Brewing Co. in Richmond, Virginia. They needn't have worried: they saw their sales shoot up by 550%, and by the end of the year twenty-three American breweries were canning.

The first canned beer to go on sale in Europe was from Welsh brewer Felinfoel. As in the US, brewers were hesitant at first, thanks to fears of lack of demand and the tainting of flavour. Felinfoel took the plunge because the family that owned the brewery also had links with a tin works just down the road in Llanelli. Their can is famous for its coned top, which tapered to a point where it could be sealed with a crown cap. (Flat-topped cans at this time all had to be opened with a can-opener or other blade.) Despite the claims of brewers, there was a taint to the flavour, and when the Second World War started brewers were banned from canning beer, apart from that sent to troops at the front, as metal was diverted to the war effort. But cans would steadily grow in prominence after the war ended.

Cans with designs printed directly onto the metal and bottles with bright, colourful, self-adhesive labels gave beer the opportunity to create colourful, attractive brands. Guinness – which had taken the firm decision not to build its own pub estate – instead pioneered funny, engaging advertising that persuaded people to ask for it by name no matter where they were drinking.

The UK's first canned beer is now its most expensive. In 2019 Philip Lewis, Manager of the Felinfoel Brewery, bought two cans at auction for £2250.

BEER AT ITS BEST
—FROM A CAN

Canned beer is better because the goodness is sealed in and the flavour preserved. It is also protected from the harmful effect of light. Unbreakable. Lighter to carry. Takes up less space. No deposits; no returns. More hygienic – used only once.

This beer will remain brilliant and in good condition for the customary period.

For most brewers, though, branding in pubs remained relatively unimportant compared to the steadily growing off-trade. Most pubs were tied to breweries and sold only their own beers. The name of the brewer would be on the sign hung outside, so you knew that if you went into a Whitbread pub you were going to get Whitbread's beers, or Courage beers in a Courage pub, and so on. Most pub estates were still highly regionalised, and the bigger brewers bought out or saw off their smaller rivals. You'd be drinking Shepherd Neame if you were in Faversham, and if you were in Edinburgh you'd be drinking Younger's. In larger cities like London or Manchester, where you may still have had a wide variety of brands to choose from, you made that choice from the name above the pub door. Most brewers brewed a similar range of beers, so once you were inside you simply asked for a pale ale, a mild or a bitter, or if you were racy, some combination thereof. This is why photographs of pubs from the early to mid-twentieth century are conspicuous by the absence of pump clips, showing naked hand pulls or hand-scribbled signs with the style of beer being served.

This began to change in the 1960s. Keg beers were served by an electric tap rather than a handpull or direct from the barrel, as cask ale was. At first, these were little plastic boxes on the bar, illuminated from within; the little red box of Watney's having a particular notoriety among drinkers old enough to remember it. Lager brands, also sold on keg, either didn't belong to the brewery that owned the pub and were sold under a licensing agreement with the foreign brewer who owned them, or they were branded by the brewer to make you think that was the case.

Gradually, branding on the bar became more important. After the 1989 beer orders, which prohibited brewers from owning more than 2,000 pubs, beer brands were free to access the whole market. Since then, brands have engaged in a steady arms race to become bigger and more noticeable on the bar, with those little plastic boxes now evolving into grand edifices of chrome and steel.

The quest for meaning and authenticity

As brands proliferated, the original guarantees of quality and authenticity they represented became commonplace. No one was seriously trying to pass off their product as someone else's – at least not in beer – and there was a growing understanding that if a brand was advertised on TV and had a wide presence in supermarkets and on pub bars, it was probably at the very least an OK example of what it was supposed to be. It might not be to your taste, but it wasn't going to kill you, and each one was going to taste pretty much like the last.

The aspects that had driven the needs for brands were now the price of entry. The fact that you had a distinctive, clear brand that drinkers could readily identify was not enough, because everyone did. Increasingly, brands sought ways not just of standing out, but of visibly differentiating themselves from all the rest.

For a long time, beer brands did this by competing to stake claims over authority, continuity and tradition. The date the brewery had been founded was mandatory, so long as it was old enough to be impressive. Often, the origin date is well-founded: the company that became Greene King was indeed founded in 1798, Shepherd Neame in 1698, Fuller's in 1845 and so on, and these foundation dates form key elements in their branding.

Where that date is not so impressive, it's still typical of brands to find the earliest evidence of brewing in the town where they are located and confuse this with how old the brand is. Thus, Stella Artois, a beer that was brewed for the first time in 1926, by a brewery that was founded in 1894, falsely claims on its packaging that it has been around since 1366, which is actually the earliest recorded date of brewing in the town of Leuven.

Symbols of royal or even religious imagery are common among older beers, as are gothic or Germanic typefaces. As well as implicitly suggesting the brand has been around since these typefaces were new and hip, these design traits can also work to suggest provenance; that this beer is really from this far-off place where they make great beer. If Teutonic heritage started to feel a bit old-hat or boring, new brands could take advantage with colours, typefaces or graphic design elements that suggested they hailed from a Mexican beach, Australian barbecue or mythical Provençal neverland.

In the 1990s, as we really got into the idea of brands as having personalities and working as carriers of emotional meaning rather than just trade marks, this worked brilliantly. Faith in traditional institutions was eroding: people no longer felt the government (of any party), the police, the Royal Family or the church could be trusted, or even that they should be. This created a trust vacuum; we needed to be able to rely on someone, and big brands – with their reassuring messages that 'you're worth it' and you can 'just do it' – filled that gap.

Briefly, we were taken in by the flash, glitz and glamour of brands that showed us a world in which we could all be living our very best lives if only we bought the right brand of disposable razor, soft drink or sanitary protection. But very quickly, we became disillusioned with what we increasingly saw as 'spin' and 'fake news'. The information explosion of the internet allowed us to see behind the scenes and below the surface, and many people began to feel that big brands, too, had betrayed our trust. Around the year 2000, with the global success of Naomi Klein's book *No Logo*, we began to learn that the big corporations behind our favourite brands were using sweatshop labour in Asia, or destroying the environment, or propping up dictators, or simply misleading us by pretending to be brewed in Germany, France or Holland when they were in fact being churned out of a warehouse just off the M4.

Two of the biggest social trends of the last twenty years have been the quest for authenticity and the search for meaningful experiences rather than just more products. A significant number of people are looking for 'the real thing' –

Stella Artois is a great example of a br... making a false claim about how long it... been brewing, in order to create a ser... permanence and reassurance. 1366 is... date of the earliest evidence of any br... in the town of Leuven, where Stella is... The Artois brewery was founded in 18...

as they always were – but now established brands that have been pushing these messages for years are no longer seen as authentic.

While we still rely on big brands for necessities such as toilet paper or batteries, an increasing number of people are seeking out smaller-scale, more localised alternatives, which they see as being more authentic, more real, simply because they operate on a more human level.

When marketing became a little too slick, slickness itself was seen by many consumers as evidence that the brand was selling empty promises. For people who felt this, a brand that looked like it had never been near a professional designer could become a virtue in itself. Many cask ale pump clips, for example, display an amateurism that seems conscious and deliberate. This is, of course, a form of marketing, a design style that instantly signals to the drinker, 'We don't have the time or money to invest in flash salesmanship. We're too busy putting everything we can into brewing great beer.'

Unfortunately, for a generation that has constantly inhaled subtle branding messages since they were born, this no longer works. Whatever a brand puts on its packaging, it sends a message to the consumer. If a brewer hasn't taken the time to think through what they want this message to be, and ensured that their branding communicates it effectively, then people are in danger of drawing conclusions from your branding that you never wanted them to:

'This beer is going to be flat and twiggy.'
'The guys who made this are a bunch of sexist pigs.'
'This brewery is out of touch with the real world and
    therefore not relevant to me.'

I doubt there's a brewery in the world that wants potential purchasers of its products to think this about them. But it happens all too often thanks to poorly thought-out or poorly-executed brand design. If you want to be visible, you don't have the option of not telling consumers what you stand for. In the absence of a clear, coherent message, they will either fail to notice you, or draw their own conclusions.

The craft beer boom

Over the last ten to fifteen years, the rules of what makes a good piece of beer design have been covered in paraffin, set alight and thrown out of the window, thanks to a band of rebels who have shaken the beer market to its foundations.

Craft beer brands began in the UK by confronting the establishment head-on. Visually, they made it very clear that they were not like the big beer brands we had known until that point. They had a different agenda, a different set of values, and at their most extreme, they were offering us a revolution. Packaging design was a big part of telling the story.

This was not just being different for the sake of it. The world had changed, and the conservative tradition of beer design was looking staid. Society had become more informal and spontaneous. Our disillusionment with brands in general was part of a broader shift, driven by the proliferation of different media channels and a fracturing of traditional, linear narratives that saw us taking a more pick and mix, sampling approach to the stories we told ourselves and the ways we interacted with the world, where we took bits from different fashions, cuisines and styles of music, and made our own looks, fusions and mixtapes.

In general, brands recognised this and tried to adapt. Following the success of Innocent Smoothies, brands across all sectors abandoned a tone of voice that might best be described as, if not parental, that of your older sister or more knowledgeable friend, and began talking to us as equals, all cutesy and informal and lower case. As packaging, pack copy and advertising voice-overs for everything from soft drinks to laundry detergent became more colloquial ('I'm lovin' it'), child-like ('yummy!' 'LOL! LMAO!') and irreverent (from 'washes whiter' to 'dirt is good') beer remained staid: it felt it had to.

In the first decade of the twenty-first century, 'binge drinking' was a moral panic, and regulations around the marketing and promotion of alcohol were being tightened. At the same time, mainstream beer had become a cheap commodity sold primarily in supermarkets on discounts. These factors combined to make beer more serious and authoritarian: bottles and cans now wagged their fingers at us telling us to drink responsibly and not to drink if pregnant, at the same time as going into overdrive on the gold and silver foil, crests and medals and cool, sober typefaces. The last thing in the world a mainstream lager wanted to appear as in the noughties was emotional or playful. In the supermarket, beer began to look less interesting visually than dog food or washing-up liquid.

This left the field wide open for craft to do something – anything – that was different; to instantly break the rules that had governed branding design and create packaging that told you in a split second that you were dealing with people who were not of the establishment and were rebelling against it.

The story we were being told in press releases and interviews was that Big Beer was bland and flavourless, whereas craft beer had more hops, more integrity, more flavour. The story we were being told on the packaging was that Big Beer was conservative and establishment, whereas craft was exuberant, energetic, colourful, playful and exciting.

At first, elements of craft beer branding shared the wilful naivety of traditional real ale design, consciously communicating an amateurism that said, 'We are anti-marketing'. But for people who were passionate about the businesses they had risked everything to set up, this couldn't last. Many craft breweries were being set up by people who were 'brand-native': who had been born into an age when encoded brand communication was everywhere. They grew up with an implicit, intuitive understanding of how branding and design worked, and didn't need a big agency to tell them how to do it. They had mates who were graphic designers or local artists, or had even had training in these areas themselves. Affordable software and digital printing made it easy to turn their designs into reality.

Then, two further developments conspired to push this explosion of design creativity even further. In 2002 American brewer Oskar Blues became the first craft brewer to actively promote cans as a premium format. It would take another ten years before the discerning beer drinker finally became convinced that cans no longer gave the beer a metallic taint. But arguments on the environmental benefits of cans – they're lighter, cheaper to transport and keep the beer fresher than bottles – eventually overcame these fears.

For young designers, cans provided a much bigger canvas to play with; an entire cylinder rather than an oval or rectangle. Clear, iconic mainstream lager brands left a lot of dead space on their cans, clean fields of blue, white or green against which the bold logo and messages could stand out. Craft set about filling that space with textures, colour washes, cartoons and secret, coded messages.

While this kind of crowded messaging could, and indeed did, create a bit of feedback-drenched noise on a supermarket shelf, this was, increasingly, not where craft beer drinkers were looking at the product. Instagram transformed social media from a word- to an image-driven environment, and the opulent Retina HD screens of new generations of smartphones made vivid colours leap out.

The revolution in beer brand design has been as dramatic as any revolution that happens where there hasn't been enough gentle evolution for far too long. The outrageous invention of pioneering craft brewers has liberated brewers of any size or longevity: visual ideas that would have looked outrageously unconventional ten years ago now sit some-where halfway between the conservatism of big brands and the novelty-seeking experimentation of small craft.

Over the last decade, beer has gone from having some of the dullest, most staid packaging in the supermarket to

having the richest, most varied, daring, occasionally the
most controversial, and sometimes the silliest, packaging
of any commercial product. Around the world, designers in
any field now look to beer for inspiration and entertainment.

Not all this experimentation has been successful, and as
we'll see, rules often exist for very good reason. But there's
never been a better time to explore great beer design: young
or old, conventional or revolutionary.

ɔllaborating with local artists to use the
ɛer can as it has never been used before,
ung brewers such as Boundary are trashing
e rules of how beer branding 'should' be done.

BREWDOG

The punks who came in from the cold

Is there any sadder sight than a middle-aged punk rocker, still trying to keep it real in bondage pants that ceased to fit long ago?

A different question: what happens when revolutionaries succeed in changing the establishment and in overthrowing the old regimes they stood against? If they carry on rebelling, what else are they supposed to destroy? If they become the new order, and embrace the responsibility that brings, does this mean they've 'sold out'?

These are different ways of approaching the problems created by spectacular commercial success. When it launched in 2007, BrewDog created fame by publicly and loudly declaring its intention to smash the status quo. Its packaging embodied

this attitude. The type is designed to give the impression that it has been badly stencilled. Like the cut-up newspaper text of punk bands from the 1970s, the individual letters don't line up with each other. It doesn't sit in the centre of the label, where convention tells you it should. The brash colours are a two-fingered salute to the conventional colour scheme of packaged beer. It's been carefully and skilfully designed to suggest it doesn't give a sh** about careful, skilful design. Nothing else in the UK beer scene looked anything like it.

By 2014 craft beer was changing the shape and look of the whole UK beer market, and BrewDog had ambitions way beyond that. The company was starting to outgrow its image of youthful rebellion, was employing hundreds of people and selling millions of bottles of beer. It wanted to grow up and mature, while still retaining its outsider status.

The 2014 redesign achieved this by shifting its focus from rebellion to craft itself. The old order had been shaken up, now it was time to lay down the principles of the new order. The dog logo has been cleaned up and made more iconic. The design was achieved by using woodcut-style textures and working with one of the last manual letterpresses in the country. The whole thing was put together without using photoshop or other computer design software. It's more grown-up, and now stands for something rather than against something.

Six years later, BrewDog felt it was time for another refresh, which met with a more mixed reception than the last. This is a brand that is now fully matured: the beers' names are clear and centred, and the shield motif is one that has been used to suggest quality beer for at least 150 years. BrewDog describe this as representing a shift from 'rebel' to 'maverick', still independent and ploughing their own furrow, but no longer standing directly against the mainstream.

BrewDog was the first new-generation craft brewer to break through and land firmly in the middle of mainstream beer. In many ways, it has transcended the craft beer category and this new design is a visual acknowledgement of the fact. It's looking to take drinkers away from Carling and Foster's rather than competing with other craft brewers, and this new design prioritises clarity and suggests familiarity.

Is it a sell-out? Well, like all punks, that depends on which aspect you bought into in the first place: the attitude or the product itself?

Instagram and the critical rehabilitation of cans as a premium format have combined to completely change the way new beers are presented to drinkers. Labels are now designed not (just) for the shelf and stand-out there, but for visual presentation on

social media. Here a Brew York and Unbarred collaboration uses three cans side-by-side to reveal the full design. The technique used here by Ora is increasingly common: using an image of a can to make it clear that we are actually looking a can of beer, but unscrolling the whole label artwork onto a flat plane to showcase it. You'd never see either brand in this way on the shelf – that's not the point. The design is to be savoured, lingered over, rather than simply to promote a flash of interest.

‘I'm lovin' it’

2

How Branding Works

The brand promise

The best way to think of a brand is as a promise, made by the manufacturer to the consumer. If you like the taste of Cadbury's chocolate, or a Big Mac, or Bass Ale, and you buy something with that logo on it, the promise being made by the logo is that the thing inside the package is going to taste exactly like the last one did, and the one before that.

That's fine if you're already a fan of the brand. But what if you've never eaten chocolate or burgers, or never tasted a beer before? How does one brand convince you to pick it up instead of the one next to it?

Advertising and marketing are of course the most straightforward ways in which manufacturers make promises to us, but a lot of decisions are made on the spur of the moment, at the bar or in front of the supermarket shelf. Here, it's all down to the packaging.

Of course, a brand has to stand out. It has to catch your eye. But it also needs – to some extent – to blend in. It has to look right. We're programmed to expect certain codes in each category. You probably wouldn't buy a beer that was packaged in the same way as bleach, and vice versa. Soft drinks come packaged in bright, dayglo colours. Ready salted crisps always have to be red, and salt and vinegar is green.

In beer, some conventions are so deeply held we rarely challenge them, or even think about them as conventions. They're just the way things are. Premium bottled ale comes in 500ml bottles. Lager comes in 330ml bottles. Why?

Because that's what we expect them to do. This rule of conforming with the norms of the category means many leading products often end up looking very similar to each other.

In the history of beer branding, the most consistent feature has been what designers refer to as the 'racetrack': the oval that goes around the front label and will contain either the name of the beer, a description of its style, or a message about the quality and premiumness of the beer. Around the world, you can spot a premium-branded flagship lager instantly, because so many of them look the same.

The usual suspects: even though the most popular beer brands vary in different parts of the world far more than they do in most product categories, mainstream category conventions are fixed and universal.

HEINEKEN

Repetition of brand name and symbol on neck to reinforce brand recognition

'Racetrack' synonymous with quality beers worldwide and maximising space on curved surface

Green bottle that looks more 'refreshing' than brown

Central brand symbol that suggests a brand-specific story or legend

Claims around passion and quality

Year established

Clear, distinct name that stands out from the pack, in bespoke, authoritative typeface

Medals and awards

Scroll device to suggest seriousness, premiumness, importance

Use of gold or silver foil to enhance premium credentials

Heineken is sold in more countries than any other beer. It has therefore been designed to look like a premium beer with codes that transcend any national cultural beer drinking tropes. Its various features and attributes are universal.

Brand personality

Over the last thirty years, the whole notion of brands has become much more nuanced. The physical mark of a brand – be it a shape, or a name written in a particular way – is merely the physical manifestation of a much bigger idea.

Thinking back to Bass, the point of the brand was that this was a guarantee of quality and consistency: that it really had been brewed by Bass. By the late twentieth century, in any walk of life, any major brand in its sector only existed because it offered the same guarantee of quality and consistency. We had our choice of brands that all offered roughly similar functional benefits. If you drink mainstream lager, you know that Foster's, Carling and Carlsberg are all pretty much the same. So brands started to implicitly promise something less tangible, but equally important. On top of the *functional* benefits of the product, they began focusing on the *emotional* benefits of the brand.

My first advertising account, in the early 1990s, was Daz laundry detergent. Procter & Gamble and Unilever between them produce pretty much all the major brands, so they differentiate slightly between each one. Daz was about whiteness, Ariel about stain removal, and so on. Then, rival Persil stole a march with commercials that went beyond 'this will clean your clothes' and addressed why this was important. Sure, lots of brands would get rid of stains, but Persil hit upon the notion that the emotional benefit of this was that it made you feel like a good mum: knowing that you were sending your kids to school looking spotless, and that they would come back scruffy, but accepting that this was

Agency United by Design piled
subtle layers of concealed detail
into their visual identity for
Brew York. 'Its significance
to the viewer is transformed
through personal interpretation
and interaction,' they say.
'They may look a little closer to
reveal the heart of its founders;
or even a skull, as a nod to
York's Gothic architecture.'

OK because that's part of being a kid. With the help of good old Persil, you'd be able to get the clothes clean again, which meant you could be a good mum twice over: giving your kids the freedom to play and get dirty, and then sorting out the washing later. Persil grew massively at the expense of brands that were still comparing stains.

This trend was even more pronounced in beer. Whereas washing powder brands can talk freely about stain removal or gleaming whites as much they like, beer brands are not allowed to talk about, or even allude to, the effects of drinking alcohol. You can say it tastes great, but all mainstream brands do, using near-identical phrases such as 'clean refreshing taste' or 'easy-drinking refreshment'. So from the 1970s, beer advertising built personalities around brands rather than trying to persuade you they simply tasted better than their competitors.

Although they've dated incredibly badly, 1970s lager ads stole a march on traditional ale by suggesting that if you were a lager drinker you were sharper and cooler than the old fogeys of the older generation. In the status-obsessed 1980s, packaging grew to play as much of a role as the ads. As designer labels spread across everything, the problem with beer was that once it had been poured into a pint glass, no one could tell what a cool brand choice you had just made. So image-conscious lager drinkers began ordering bottled beer instead, paying almost as much money for just over half as much beer as you got in a pint, and drinking straight from the bottle, the label turned carefully outward, so everyone could see what you were drinking.

The main tool used by designer beer was provenance. If you drank Australian lager, that suggested you shared their laid-back, 'no worries' attitude. If you drank Corona or Sol, it was a bit easier to pretend you were partying on a beach in Mexico rather than a nightclub in Blackpool.

With any great brand, the mark becomes valuable and meaningful because the feelings and meanings we associate with it are valuable. The Nike swoosh on its own means nothing. But for millions around the globe, every time they see it they think of athletic excellence.

In small businesses, we put a value on this implicit meaning and call it 'goodwill'. It's the value in the business that can't be measured in terms of stock or property, but still contributes to commercial success. When it's measured for big brands, it's worth colossal amounts. The most valuable brand in the world is Amazon, which is worth $220 billion. That's an awful lot of goodwill.

It may sound ludicrous to suggest that brands have personalities. If you were asked in a supermarket whether the packet of biscuits in your hand was optimistic or pessimistic, friendly or aloof, thoughtful or carefree, you might wonder about the sanity of the person questioning you. But in market research focus groups, it's common to ask a question along the lines of 'If this brand was a person, and it came into the room right now, what kind of person would it be?'

Respondents can always answer, and their answers are almost always consistent. Some of our projection of brand personality is based on the kind of person who we think drinks them: real ale brands always come to life as someone a little older; craft beers are embodied as younger drinkers with facial hair and tattoos. But there are nuances that go

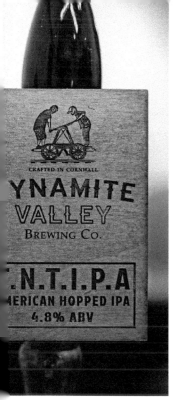

Brands express their personalities in a number of different ways, some obvious, some subtle. Dynamite Valley make a bold statement about their Cornish provenance, then add other cues via materials, typefaces, illustration style, even the way they photograph their brands.

beyond that. A brand that people really admire often comes to life as someone similar to you, but slightly cooler, more knowledgeable or capable: an older brother or someone who has travelled the world a bit more. When people describe their favourite lager brand, it's invariably the coolest person in a group of drinkers in the pub. Whether that translates as the person who has the best jokes, the person who always buys the first round, or the person who has the most stylish clothes depends on the brand you're talking about.

If brands have personalities, then we judge each other by the company we keep. This is nothing new. People have always acquired swords, horses, estates or even countries not only for their functional benefits, but also because of what they projected about that person. We've always used objects as talismans that project an image of ourselves, but also to change things inwardly; to change how we feel about ourselves.

Packaging communicates the values and personality of a brand in some ways that are obvious, and others that are so subtle they can seem like magic or hypnotism. Certain colours, certain typefaces, can suggest freshness, authenticity, premiumness, or good value. Some of these cues are pretty near the surface: put a lot of gold foil on a pack and you're clearly trying to suggest this is a premium product. Others are deeply hidden, and not entirely explainable.

There's a science to this: the science of how signs work. Semiotics works on the logic that a meaningful sign has two components: the signifier – a physical word, object, sound, colour or symbol – and the signified; a mental concept or meaning. While signifiers might change little over time, the signified concept – the meaning of the sign – is determined by culture, history and context. A red rose means romance. But the colour red in a cross might signify medical help. Draw that red cross differently, and it's a flag that could mean English patriotism, far right racism or the Christian persecution of Muslims, depending on where it is, and who you are. In beer, green bottles signify freshness. Abstract textures on cans signify craft. Embossing on bottles or pump clips signify premium quality.

Semiotics runs deeper than those obvious surface cues, and to 'read' semiotic cues in full requires a bit of training. But when they're pointed out to us, they usually make sense to the novice: we kind of knew these cues were there and we were picking up on them and responding to them. We just couldn't readily articulate them.

But there's a third layer of meaning in how we respond to branding and design which goes even deeper, one that is only just starting to be understood.

Professor Charles Spence runs the Crossmodal Research Laboratory at Oxford University. He explores the way in which different senses interact, help and often confuse each other, and a lot of the work he does is in the food and drink industries. His endlessly fascinating experiments reveal that a dessert will taste sweeter on a round, white plate, and more bitter on a square black slate. A heavier bottle can make a beer seem more premium, which is an issue for manufacturers who are under pressure to reduce the weight of packaging to make their product more sustainable. However, Spence's research shows that we perceive darker, more saturated colours as 'heavier', and paler colours as 'lighter'. So you can make a beer feel more premium by making it feel heavier, and you can make it feel heavier by saturating the colours more deeply. If you have a soft drink in a green can, you can make that drink 'taste' more lemony by imperceptibly increasing the percentage of yellow in the shade of green. Or you can make it 'taste' sweeter by switching to red packaging instead.

Some of this may sound sinister – and some designers are adept at using visual cues to get us to think something without our being aware of it – but most people have a surprisingly high level of brand literacy. In general, we understand how brand design works, and we use it to help navigate our choices at the bar, shelf or screen. Design is an incredibly efficient way of transferring not just information but also emotional signals between producer and consumer.

BARNEY'S BEER

Barney's is a microbrewery and distillery located at Summerhall in Edinburgh, a former medical school that now serves as one of the key venues of the Edinburgh Science Festival. For the 2014 Festival, Barney worked with Professor Charles Spence of the Crossmodal Research laboratory to explore the impact of labelling on people's beer preferences. Three beers were presented to drinkers: one in plain packaging, one with a brown label and one with a green label. After tasting each beer when poured from the bottler and served in a glass, they were asked to score the beers on a scale of one to nine in its taste, quality, citrus flavour, the likelihood that they would buy it, and the price they'd be prepared to pay for it.

On each measure (except price) the beer with the green label scored higher than the other two, particularly on citrus flavour and purchase intent. On most scores, the beer with the brown label came second, except for citrus flavour, where it came a distant third behind both the green and plain bottles.

The beer in each bottle was identical, from the same brew, on the same day, with the labels applied after the beer had been bottled.

Protecting brands

Successful branding, therefore, consists of a bunch of different elements which designers and marketers now refer to as 'assets'. It's a relatively recent application of the word, and when I first heard it, it caused the same gag reflex I often get when marketers mangle and abuse innocent words for their own nefarious ends. But thinking about it, it's a perfectly accurate word to use for the collection of colours, shapes, images and typefaces that make up the look and feel of a brand, and which together denote its origin, nature and personality. An asset is defined as either a useful or desirable thing, or an item of ownership that has exchangeable value. Brand 'assets' fit both definitions. They are items of value because they are items of great power, and they therefore have to be carefully protected.

One form of protection is legal. Apart from luxury brands such as Rolex or Luis Vuitton, straightforward fake branding is rare these days. But lawsuits over 'passing off' a brand as someone else's are frequent. This usually takes the form of visual assets being used in a way that makes a cheap brand look like a more established one, at least at first glance. For a gallery of examples of what this looks like, simply check out the beer fixture at Aldi or Lidl.

But valuable brand assets need protecting internally too. They work when used in a particular way, following specific rules. Big brands will lay these rules down in a brand book, often referred to as a 'brand bible': what is the exact shade of red? What is the minimum size of the logo? Can you reverse that logo out so it's white on black, or not? Brand books ensure

(right) Brand books or brand 'b[...] detail exactly how each element[...] brand identity must be used, to[...] consistent application whereve[...] brand is seen by consumers.

Brand Guidelines

Logo

The positioning of our primary logo is within a circle. Use our second Sun-circled logo in certain situations.

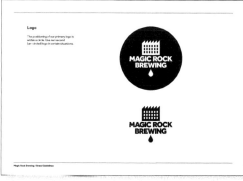

Logo colour options

Only use our logo in solid black or reversed out white.

Logos are available to download from magicrockbrewing.com/logos

Logo usage - position

Do not stretch, squash, slant, delete, drip, shade or drop shadow our logo.

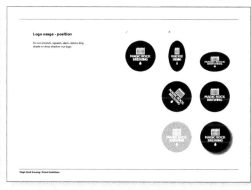

Typefaces

Primary Typeface

The primary typeface for Magic Rock Brewing is Effra. Please use this guide for correct typesetting.

Effra regular - Used for body copy
The quick brown fox jumps over the lazy dog

Effra medium - Used for sub headings
The quick brown fox jumps over the lazy dog

Effra bold - Used for headings
The quick brown fox jumps over the lazy dog

Effra heavy - Used for beer names
The quick brown fox jumps over the lazy dog

Office Typeface

Our website had Effra integrated into the site however for email, please use Helvetica or Arial depending on your system fonts.

Helvetica - Used for email
The quick brown fox jumps over the lazy dog

Logo safe area

When using our logo, please allow enough space. For correct spacing, please use the hight of the factory as a guide.

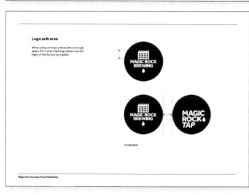

Acceptable

Photography

If you require photos* please contact our Marketing Manager.

These should not be edited.

*Magic Rock own the images and they may not be reproduced, copied, transmitted or manipulated without the written permission of Magic Rock.

©2015 Magic Rock Brewing. All rights reserved.

Graphics

If you require graphics for your event, please request these by email to: info@magicrockbrewing.com

Please, do not edit our graphics.

that the effectiveness of the design is not compromised in the hands of, say, someone knocking up a quick leaflet or a local magazine.

Brands have come a long way since Bass registered its triangle to prevent other people from using it. How do you effectively define something that is both a physical mark, a set of visual assets, a differentiated product, an implicit promise, a personality and a set of values? My favourite definition of a brand was coined by ad exec Paul Feldwick in his 1991 book *Understanding Brands*. Feldwick defined a brand simply as 'A collection of meanings commonly held by people'. It's particularly useful because it carries a warning to anyone who sells a brand. You might have a PowerPoint document somewhere that says what you want your brand to be, but once it's out there in the world, that might not be the meaning other people imbue it with. If you think your lager is a beer of supreme quality and value, but millions of people think of it as 'wifebeater', then that is the meaning of your brand, and you have a huge job on your hands to change that perception. Similarly, any brewer who insists 'We don't believe in marketing' is running a huge risk. If your beer hasn't been noticed, it's not going to sell and you're going to go out of business. If it has been noticed, then people out there are forming a collection of meanings around it. It's far better for your business if you're exercising a degree of control over what those meanings might be. And if you're doing that, whether you're buying TV ads or just taking care to get the tone and content of your tweets right, then you're engaging in brand marketing.

PILOT

Pilot was founded in Leith, Edinburgh, in 2013 by Matt Johnson and Patrick Jones. Matt's previous career was in graphic design, so all the brand development for Pilot was done in-house.

Pilot's beers have always been unfined and therefore hazy. Commonplace now, this was unusual in Edinburgh in 2013, so a clean, minimalist, professional-looking design scheme was chosen as a way of reassuring drinkers that the beer inside was meant to be like that. It was also designed to stand out and be clearly identifiable in a dark, busy bar. While there's enough flair and quirkiness to make it look like a craft beer, the packaging still conforms to classic commercial branding rules – and that's why it still works. 'We wanted to create something that had longevity and very little about our branding has changed in our seven-or-so years of trading,' says Matt. 'We've seen other breweries rebrand two or three times since we started, so this is something we're pretty proud of.'

MAGIC ROCK

Pulling off great brand-building tricks

Synaesthesia is condition whereby people experience sensory information with the wires crossed: sounds can be perceived to have colours; numerals or letters might have tastes; or different words may be perceived as having different odours. Neuroscientists are still struggling to fully understand it, with some arguing as few as 1 in 100,000 experiences it, and others suggesting that we are all somewhere on a scale, all capable of being pushed into sensory overlap and feedback.

It's something Magic Rock founder Richard Burhouse wanted to embed deeply into his branding design. 'When we started, I was a big fan of American craft beer design,' he says. 'Brands like 3 Floyds were original and idiosyncratic. They appealed to you on a deep level without you really being able to understand why.'

With ambitions to become a significant national player in craft beer, Burhouse wanted to avoid the geographical limitation of a name such as 'Huddersfield Brewery'. The family business sold crystals and rocks, so 'Magic Rock' felt like a name with a story that could stretch to suggest a whole lot more. Again avoiding an obvious route such as giving beers names like 'Amethyst Pale Ale', Burhouse focused instead on the 'Magic' part, and came up with the vision of a circus sideshow: fun, but with a bit of darkness. The core range included beers with names like 'High Wire' and 'Human Cannonball', and were brought to life in the world of a circus big top, with strongmen, bearded ladies and helter-skelters bursting out from pump clips and bottle labels onto vans and beer mats, even manifesting in the shape of co-founder and head brewer

Stuart Ross hosting beer launches in a black-and-white leotard that, once seen, could never be erased from the retinas. 'It all fit together,' says Burhouse. 'The names, the imagery, the style of illustration. I wanted you to be able to look at the packaging and somehow *taste* the beer from it, to know what it was going to be like, like synaesthesia.'

In 2017, as the craft beer world moved on and Burhouse grew apprehensive about a call from industry watchdog the Portman Group (in fact, the call never came) it was time to move the design on. A seasonal launch called Fantasma had packaging designed by the same artist as the launch range, a young graphic designer called Richard Norgate, whose work Burhouse had spotted on an album cover for the Arctic Monkeys. ('I found it very appealing without really knowing why.') Following the

convention that limited beers could be more daring, the design for Fantasma was much more abstract, shapes and colours rather than recognisable characters. The beer was so popular that it ended up becoming part of the core range. 'When that happened, we had no option but to redesign the rest of the core range to fit with it,' says Burhouse.

In my mind's eye, the redesign shows us close-up details of the Magic Rock's dark and mysterious circus sideshow. But looking closely at the illustrations now, there is no recognisable detail: it still feels like the circus, but in an abstract, synaesthetic, impressionistic way. Hopefully, this means we'll never have to worry about seeing Stu in his leotard ever again.

It's hard to think of a brand more visually diverse than Pressure Drop. With photography, illustration, abstract patterns and cartoons, they make a point of trashing any notion of consistent visual identity. And yet, every single one of these cans is instantly recognisable as a Pressure Drop beer because of clean, consistent placement of logos and type.

3

Brand
Architecture

Happy families

If a company makes more than one product, it has to decide how its various products sit together and relate to each other, and what to prioritse in terms of branding. Should they look like part of a family? Should each separate product have its own, distinct identity? Is the 'brand' the name of the company, or just the name of the product itself?

The correct approach depends on variety of factors, and what is 'correct' in terms of marketing theory doesn't always happen. Branding can be a messy business. You probably buy a whole bunch of household products without being aware of whether they are all made either by Unilever or Procter & Gamble. But you probably refer to your car by the name of its manufacturer rather the serial number or model: it's an Audi or a Mercedes rather than an A3 or a B-Class. But rules are variable: if it's a Volkswagen, you may think of it as Volkswagen, or as a Polo or Beetle.

It can get more complicated when a product range evolves over time. Different variants come and go. When you launch a new product, do you launch it as an extension of an existing brand or as a new brand in its own right?

There is a theory to doing it right. If someone already buys one of your products to do one thing, they're already invested in your brand and trust it, so it probably makes sense to use the equity you've already built up. You don't have to go to the trouble of coming up with a new name and identity, and you've got more chance of getting the brand listed for sale by outlets already stocking your original brand. However, if you're aiming the new product at a completely different target audience, it might make more sense to launch it under a new brand name.

The other variable to consider, apart from whether you're targeting the same people or different people, is whether you're offering the same benefit or a different benefit. If you're offering a range of products with similar benefits to the same people – say, bags of crisps with different flavours – it makes sense to have them as variants within the same brand. But if you're a company that makes crisps and snacks and you want to offer low-fat variants, you might launch them as a sub-brand, or a clearly defined variant of the main brand. If you want to launch a range of vegan meals, there's little value in using your main brand. It may even harm you: if people know you for tasty but fattening treats, maybe they'll be less likely to believe your vegan meals are healthy than if you launched them under a new brand.

Commercial, personal and political pressures get in the way. I was once involved in a major branding project in Eastern Europe where the brand manager of a big mainstream macro lager wanted to launch a range of 'craft' beers. I pointed out that the brand was so strongly associated with macro lager that he would be far better off removing its name from the new beers, and that the brewery owned other brands

Burton brewer Marston's has acquired various breweries over the years, and developed sub-ranges of its own, and now presides over dozens of different beer brands – far more than we can show here. Decision-making how these beers should fit toget – or not – is a constant process.

that would be a far better fit for these new beers. In return, he pointed out that his job was to be the brand manager of the macro lager brand, and if the new beers were launched under a different brand, they wouldn't belong to him. Of course, the beers never ended up launching.

If that sounds absurd or extreme, similar things happen all the time. In Big Beer, brand managers typically work in a position for around two years before moving onto another role, and they want to get something in their CV during that time. Decisions are taken for short-term effect with little thought given to how new launches and brand extensions can divide resources, confuse the consumer and generally muddy the waters on what the brand stands for.

In beer, most brewers offer a range of different beers aimed at a broadly similar target market. This means there's usually a need to build a reputation for the brewery itself. Sometimes this name may be synonymous with a single beer, or there may be one beer within a range that stands out as a flagship. The relationship between the brewery name and the names of individual beers creates some common permutations which provide a useful way to look at the range, or 'brand architecture' of what a brewer offers.

Single beer brand

Think of the biggest beer brands in the world, and they tend
to be fairly monolithic. If your business focus is mainstream
lager, there's not much point in having a bunch of different
variants beyond the main and 'lite' variants of lager brands
in the US. Carlsberg and Heineken are the names of massive
breweries that produce a wide range of beer brands. But
they are also the names of individual beers that are the
most famous products these companies make. There's no
apparent brand relationship between, say, Heineken and
Amstel, or Carlsberg and Tuborg. They may be owned by
the same company, but as brands they're quite separate.

These big, stand-alone brands compete directly against
each other, so the aim of branding design is to make them
iconic and highly recognisable, working across different
cultures and language barriers. They're often photographed
from below, so we're looking up at the label, the 330ml
bottle standing, often against a black background, like
the mysterious monolith from *2001: A Space Odyssey*.

In recent years, many of these brands seem to have started
to take themselves a little too seriously in their attempts to
shore up their 'quality' and 'premium' credentials. They do
this at their peril: big beer brands are meant to be friendly
and approachable – that's the essence of what beer is –
and claiming to be 'The king of beers' or telling drinkers
in a finger-wagging fashion that 'It's a chalice, not a glass'
risks coming across as arrogant and aloof.

CARLSBERG

Carlsberg had fallen behind some of its competitors in the UK, struggling to shift an increasingly widespread image as the archetypal 'cooking lager': cheap, weak, and lacking in character. In 2018 a new rebrand was introduced as part of a wholesale reinvention that boldly acknowledged how people perceived it, and ultimately led to a completely new recipe.

Compared to the conventions of macro lager branding, Carlsberg is now striking in its simplicity, suggesting a real sense of self-confidence without arrogance. The logo – which was always supposed to be a hop leaf – now looks a bit more like one. The green is slightly lighter and fresher. The logo is instantly recognisable and familiar, but has been redrawn and is now softer and friendlier than it was. Big brands have to change incrementally, and for a brand the size of Carslberg this award-winning redesign is a bold and confident statement that makes an old brand feel a good deal more contemporary.

Variants first, with house name reassurance

Established brewers rarely sit down with a masterplan and design an entire range of beers from scratch. Names might be changed to reflect changing trends. A beer that starts off as a seasonal may prove so popular it ends up becoming permanent. A brewer might buy a rival and acquire popular beers that are too established to change but don't fit with the existing scheme. One beer might become wildly more popular than the others, and account for the lion's share of sales: many brewers with a broad range of beers have one particular beer that might be worth of up 80% of their total sales. How do you give that beer room to breathe while at the same time supporting the rest?

There is no single right answer to these questions, and every brewer's portfolio is quite different. Greene King has bought various other brewers over the years. As well as having a range of Greene King beers it also owns brands such as Ridley's, Morland and Hardy & Hanson, some of which have branded beers of their own. Gradually these are losing their distinctiveness and are all being drawn under the Greene King umbrella. Marston's has also acquired other brewers, but has gone to great lengths to preserve their distinct regional identities.

If there is an approach that's consistent, it tends to be one that could be described as a 'house of brands': each beer stands alone with an independent identity, with the brewery's name in the background as a quiet reassurance of quality.

FULLER'S

Fuller's is a great example of a range of brands that is a bit of a mixed bag. London Pride is far bigger than any other beer, a bona fide brand in its own right that stands in a similar fashion to a Carlsberg or a Heineken. But at the same time, 'Pride' is part of a broad family of beers. In its marketing, Fuller's is continually torn between trying to promote the Fuller's brand name as it works across the entire range, or focusing on building their flagship brand and hope that other brands can bathe in some reflected glory.

Comparing the brands to each other, there's barely any consistency: each one has to work on its own. While the labels on the bottles are all rectangular, many of them feature the racetrack oval, but not all. On the bar, the pump clips are all different shapes. There's no clear visual relationship between London Pride, ESB and Wild River. Some beers, such as Bengal Lancer, are given specific brand names, whereas others, like London Porter, are just described by their style.

This is why it's important to have a clear and consistent Fuller's logo across all beers, with the griffon being the only visual element all the beers have in common.

Themed range identity within house style

Some beer ranges are designed in such a way that while each beer remains an independently named brand, there's also a strong family resemblance. This can take the form of a unifying common shape, or frame, in which different names and pictures can sit. The names and picture themselves may all be different, but they might have a common theme, or obviously come from the same artist, or have other elements in common such as a theme uniting the names.

The advantage of this approach is that while each beer can work just fine on its own, the range together is more than the sum of its parts. If you adore one beer with a particular visual identity or style purely on its own merits, and then discover that it's part of a bigger range with similarly attractive members of the family, this helps build the brewery's reputation on a broader scale. When it's done right, a beer might look great on its own, but it looks even better when it's part of a range.

As with the 'house of brands' approach above, it's rare to find an established brewery that's had this approach all neatly worked out from the start, with each new beer feeding into a growing picture. Some new brewers have done this to great effect – so far – but for many others it's more common to achieve the same result by undertaking a rebrand (see page 79) and retro-fitting an established range of beers that may have grown haphazardly over time into a newly tidied-up architecture.

BADGER

The 2018 redesign for Badger Ales is a perfect example of how diverse brands can be given a greater degree of house style. Badger is brewed by Hall & Woodhouse, a long and cumbersome name compared to 'Badger'. Selling the beers under the name 'Badger' also evokes the company's countryside roots.

The brewery has long produced a wide range of beers that each carry an individual name: Hopping Hare, Fursty Ferret, Blandford Fly, and so on. Now, each carries the Badger logo on a neck label, and the visual design of the main labels has been redone so that while each retains a distinct personality, they do look like part of a family. When you see them together, you get more of a sense that each one is telling a different story about Badger's Dorset heritage.

THORNBRIDGE

Thornbridge's current design aesthetic has gradually become more 'craft' without slavishly following design trends. Each new beer in the range is still named independently, with no relationship to any other, but the visual design is consistent across the range. The combination suggests that each beer is different in personality, but all share the same high standards of quality.

Brewery brand first with range of variants

This option is particularly popular among modern craft brewers. Rather than pushing a particular beer, the brewery wants its name to be known as a house of good beer above and beyond anything else.

The craft beer segment moves far quicker than the rest of the beer market. A brewery that has ideas to stay the course will be well aware that, over time, certain beer styles will rise and fall in popularity. As the core line-up of beers may well change over time, there's less value and much more risk in trying to build individual brand personalities into each one. By building all the equity into the brewery brand, there's a freedom to brew any beer, and an expectation that a broad number of styles will be explored.

The personality as expressed by design is the personality of the brewery itself, probably saying at least as much about the story and values of the people who run it as it does about any beer they will brew. It also works out much cheaper and more efficient than trying to build an identity for each beer in turn.

Variants may get individual names, but even if they do they'll exist within a fixed template with little visual difference between styles. It's common that instead of names they may only need to be described by style: pale ale, lager, porter, IPA and so on.

FIVE POINTS

Five Points launched in Hackney, East London, in 2013. At that time, craft brewing was exploding in London, with new breweries opening every few weeks. It was difficult to keep track of who was who in a blizzard of new brand identities.

Five Points launched with a modest core range and built a solid reputation for quality and consistency over wild experimentation. With that reputation in place, it could transfer that promise to newer, quirkier beers.

The brand design helped establish this reputation by being clear, simple and rigidly consistent. All the core beers are variations on the same design template. They communicate first and foremost that this is a beer from the Five Points Brewery, with the beer style coming second. Occasionally there is some atypical concession to naming (Hook Island Red, Railway Porter) but even here, the template and colour scheme is rigid across the entire range, creating a strong house style.

Seven Brothers have a good, distinctive name, with a story behind it to match (they really are seven brothers), so it's highly appropriate that their range looks like a bunch of different, noisy members of the same family.

mart use of type creates a simple yet distinctive look that can work across a range and looks better the more amples there are in a line-up. The variation in colour is the only concession given to different beer styles.

Exale's core range is reminiscent of a page from a stamp collection, where it's common to see a single image reproduced in different colours for different values, giving a pleasing rainbow effect when the full range is seen together.

Sub-brands

When you have a strong brand that stands for something clear and distinctive, it can be tempting to use the equity in that brand to give a leg-up to a brand-new launch. If people think Nike makes the best trainers in the world, they'll be much more likely to buy Nike sports socks, but what if Nike wanted to launch an energy drink?

Ninety per cent of new brand launches fail. If that new launch was an extension of an existing brand, that failure could damage the reputation of the parent brand too. Sometimes the problem is stretching the parent brand too far beyond what it's known to be famous for: Nike may be experts on sport, but what do they know about drinks? Other times, it might be that they're stretching too far beyond their core target audience. How many people who drink energy drinks actually play sport?

The answer can often be a sub-brand: an offshoot or sequel to the main brand. This provides a kind of background endorsement from a brand that is recognised as having some expertise in the field, but acknowledges that the core promise of the main brand might not be 100% relevant in this particular case, and that this should be made clear to the consumer with a degree of differentiation.

ADNAMS

Adnams is respected as a traditional brewer of cask ales that shares several attributes with modern craft beer – small-scale, localised production, quality ingredients and traditional techniques – but looks very different from craft beers on the bar or shelf. Venerable brewers trying to speak the language of modern craft are always in danger of committing the sin of 'dad dancing', as if they are suffering a midlife crisis.

Adnams solved this conundrum elegantly by looking to the past. They discovered the 'Jack' brand (right) in the company archives, and realised that with a little brushing up, it suddenly looked contemporary and quirky (below) and provided a perfect sub-brand under which to launch a range of more adventurous, 'crafty' beers that was true to the company's heritage but visually differentiated from its core range (below right).

Mixing it up

Another way that portfolios can be divided up is between a core range and limited editions or variable beers. The core range needs to work in the way any brand does, promising consistency and reliability. This is balanced by the novelty of limited-edition beers. Traditional real ale brewers often have a programme of seasonal beers throughout the year, and real ale drinkers will often look at a range of hand pumps in search for something they haven't had before. Modern craft has accelerated this process, with many breweries seeming to supply a constant stream of new products.

It's common practice to create a visual difference between the core range and seasonal or limited beers. The core range will often be more conservative, and simpler in design. Occasional beers can have a bit more fun and take a few risks. The design could consist of anything, and names will often be outlandish as they're trying to attract attention in the short term rather than building lasting equity.

In traditional real ale, this is where you often see puns, jokes and cartoons, the idea being that asking for a pint of Old Leghumper or 99 Red Baboons will raise a good-natured titter at the bar.

Craft beer does its own version of this, but in quite a different way. Instead of using humour, it might deploy mystery and subtlety. Breweries may badge their core range in a fairly straightforward way, but then symbolise their guest or limited-edition beers by being far more oblique.

BRICK

Peckham's Brick Brewery is built around a core 'foundation' range and takes influences from European and American beer styles. It's rigidly simple in its look and feel, with a textured brickwork effect on the finish that makes it feel reassuring and solid: important if you want people to think that you have consistent brewing skill across a broad range of styles.

The limited editions and seasonals throw all of this in a skip, favouring abstract, geometric patterns that suggest fruitiness, which is a common feature of many of the hazy IPAs and fruit sours therein.

The core range sets up a relatively new brewery with the solidity to establish itself in the long term, while the seasonals allow it to play in whatever creative space craft beer happens to be obsessing over at any given time.

FULL CIRCLE

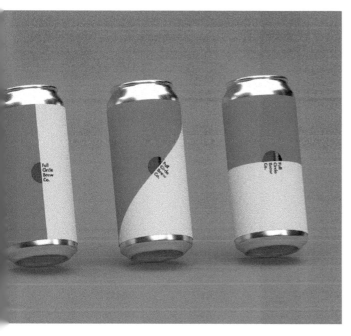

Often, a brand architecture can run into difficulty when the brewery's adventures take it in different directions than they initially envisaged. New styles of beer may not fit into the original structure, and the range can start to look messy and confused.

Full Circle, founded in Newcastle in 2019, created a simple graphic design scheme that promises unlimited flexibility. The core, permanent range of beers are each inspired by the brewery's location and foundation story. Graphics alluding to these aspects are on one half of the design, with a diagonal line separating them from clean white space where the beer name, brewery logo and information about the beer all sit.

Seasonal and limited-edition beers follow a similar logic, but these are differentiated from the core range by a line that is vertical rather than diagonal. Finally, when the brewery does a collaboration, the design features a horizontal separation of the different elements. It may be simple, but it's a strong and clever device.

Mothership has an all-female brewery team committed to the idea of 'beer for all'.
The design for the core range is energetic and inclusive, and then the specials range celebrates
'Extraordinary Women' who have broken down boundaries and stood up for women's rights.
The first release depicts Joan Clarke, a crypto-analyst who helped crack the Enigma Code in
the Second World War. The powerful image aims to draw people in to find out more.

Collaborations

Nothing demonstrates the unique collegiate nature of craft brewing compared to other markets as much as the collaboration brew. Brands in any sector are, technically, competitors. It's common for people working for them to be heated rivals who struggle to even speak to each other. While craft brewers do compete for the same bar space and the same drinkers, they are also united by a shared identity as underdogs, fighting for a cause as well as a business, and stronger together in the struggle against corporate brewing monoliths.

Collaboration brews usually feature brewers from one brewery hosting brewers from another as guests. Often they will be brewers from different markets or countries, so the competition between the two is less direct. Smaller brewers might collaborate with bigger organisations, trading credibility and hype for bigger batches and greater commercial reach. The two sets of brewers will swap recipe ideas beforehand, and good-natured rivalry will usually result in beers being a little more out there than the normal core range.

The visual design of a collaboration brew will usually follow the style of the host brewer, but will always feature the branding of the guest too. Seeing the logos of two different brewers on the same can, bottle or pump clip brings home just how exceptional this practice is in the cut-throat world of business.

CLOUDWATER

In 2019 Cloudwater launched its first 'Friends & Family & Beer' festival, celebrating the spirit of independence it shared with other breweries around the world. As well as inviting a range of craft breweries to pour their beer, they invited a selection of them to brew collaboration beers especially for the festival.

The textural designs are slightly more playful than normal, and much of the structural elements that normally shape Cloudwater's design template are missing. The whole point is that this is a collaboration between two (or more!) breweries. That's the story being told here. So the logos of the breweries involved, given equal weight on the design, tell that story perfectly all on their own.

The rebrand

Everybody needs a makeover from time to time, especially brands that rely on being contemporary and up-to-the minute: nothing dates as fast as fashion.

Even brands that you think haven't changed since you were a kid are undergoing a steady evolution to ensure they remain relevant and contemporary without sacrificing their core identity. Sometimes a brand does lose its way; becomes too flash, too cheap or too self-obsessed, and needs a brand refresh to rediscover its true self.

A rebrand isn't just about staying up-to-date: it can also be employed to sorting out all the mess and loose ends that growth creates, tidying up a diverse, scattered portfolio of beers and giving them a new, common visual identity.

Like the best haircut you ever had or the best new piece of clothing you ever bought, the best rebrands are not about trying to look hipper or younger than you really are: they're about rediscovering and re-expressing your true identity.

In a market that's as dynamic as craft beer, the rebrand is an increasingly important tool. In researching this book, about a dozen of the breweries we contacted to say we loved their design and wanted to feature it replied that they had already ditched it for a new design that was (sometimes, but by no means always) even better.

Harvey's Brewery was founded in Lewes, East Sussex, in 1790, and has been brewing on its current site since 1838. Unusually for a brewery these days, it sits right in the heart of the town of Lewes and is known affectionately by locals as 'Lewes Cathedral'.

A 2016 rebrand gave Harvey's a fresh new look that felt contemporary without sacrificing any of the brewery's traditional cues. The bright colour scheme is intended to evoke the chalk cliffs of Sussex contrasting with the ozone-bright sky of England's south coast.

TIMOTHY TAYLOR'S

Timothy Taylor's is an award-winning brewery with a cult following that is built on a simple commitment to hard work. The relationship between 'craft', as in the notion of 'craftsmanship', and 'craft' as in cool, funky beer is a curious one. You can demonstrate the epitome of craftsmanship in brewing, and yet not be perceived as a 'craft brewer' because you are too old and staid (right). The 2018 rebrand of Timothy Taylor's core range was an attempt to close a gap that shouldn't really exist in the first place: a new design that would attract younger craft drinkers without alienating the older core drinkers who were already wedded to the brand.

The creative inspiration was communist propaganda posters from the 1920s and 1930s which portrayed the ordinary labourer as a hero. Each beer champions a master tradesperson striking a pose that reflects the craftsmanship of their trade and the care and effort that goes into to making the beer, creating a nicely unified theme across the core range (below).

VOCATION

Getting it right, then making it better

Vocation launched in 2015 in the West Yorkshire town of Hebden Bridge. Founder John Hickling had previously run Nottingham's Blue Monkey, a brewer of well-respected traditional real ales. Vocation was to be anything but traditional. From the start, the brewery aimed to be a leading light of the craft beer revolution, borrowing the attitude of BrewDog and Beavertown, but carefully creating their own version of bold beers with a renegade personality.

The brand identity was created by Robot Food, a Leeds-based design agency, and it got everything right. The core range of beers featured a visual design that managed to be intricate without being over-complicated. It looked impactful from a distance, but

offered some rewarding close-up detail. The line-drawn illustrations vary from can to can, dropping hints about the character of the beer inside, and evoking contemporary cultural cues from prison tats to pirates. The beers each had their own brand names, but all followed the same format: 'Heart & Soul', 'Bread & Butter', 'Life & Death'. The core range therefore managed to pull off the neat trick where every Vocation beer had its own unique name and personality, while at the same time every Vocation beer looked exactly like every other Vocation beer.

Vocation then took the unusual step – for a small craft brewery – of making distribution in supermarkets their number one priority. As a business decision, this was an astonishing

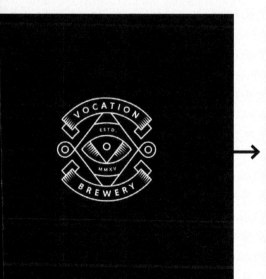

success: the brand grew from zero to being worth £7 million in the space of four years, making it one of the off-trade's biggest craft beer brands.

This success brought new challenges, and in 2019 Robot Food did a subtle refresh of the brand. While the cans were highly distinctive, it was less than clear who the brewery behind them was. With the focus now being on densely crowded supermarket shelves, it was felt more could be done to make them really stand out. Finally, Vocation wanted to introduce a range of monthly limited-edition cans that needed to stand out as something very different, yet still look like they came from Vocation.

The answer was subtle simplification. The Vocation logo was stripped down to its core element and made bigger. The detail of the design was simplified but not dumbed down side-by-side, the difference between old and new is dramatic, yet when you see the new designs on their own you can hardly tell the difference. The core range now stands out far more strongly on a cluttered supermarket shelf. It's much clearer who the brewer is, but the design has lost none of its attitude.

For the limited-edition beers, Robot Food developed a rigid template incorporating the revised logo. But this template leaves enough space for pretty much any visual design to be plastered across it. This allows Vocation to go anywhere they want in terms of individual, one-off designs, while never straying from a clear brand architecture.

'think different'

4

Lettering and Typography

| MORE | ART | THAN | BEER |

| ABSTRAKT | % | | |

| | BEER | ½ | |

| % | 500 | ML | |

| 12% | ABV | | A |

| ð | ABSTRAKT | X | LIQUORICE |

| ART | THAN | BEER | B |

| S | % | | ABV |

There's more to type than you think

Good packaging typography speaks to us simultaneously in two different languages, each communicating important information.

The first language is the one we're reading in, and it's telling us a story about the brand, or information about the product. In her excellent book *Why Fonts Matter*, typographer Sarah Hyndman shows how the second language is embedded in the shapes, sizes and positions of the letters: it tells us extra information about the personality of the brand, and is understood implicitly and emotionally.

This deeper, embedded meaning in typography goes back at least as far as the illuminated manuscripts that were painstakingly copied by medieval monks. While 'illumination' strictly refers to the illustration and decoration around the text, monks were expected to follow commonly agreed letter shapes rather than simply write in neat handwriting. These letter shapes were meant to convey the importance and solemnity of the text, and they changed from country to country, and over time. The overall style is known as blackletter.

𝔚𝔥𝔢𝔫 𝔍𝔬𝔥𝔞𝔫𝔫𝔢𝔰 𝔊𝔲𝔱𝔢𝔫𝔟𝔢𝔯𝔤 𝔦𝔫𝔳𝔢𝔫𝔱𝔢𝔡 𝔱𝔥𝔢 𝔣𝔦𝔯𝔰𝔱 𝔪𝔬𝔳𝔞𝔟𝔩𝔢 𝔱𝔶𝔭𝔢 𝔭𝔯𝔦𝔫𝔱𝔦𝔫𝔤 𝔭𝔯𝔢𝔰𝔰, 𝔱𝔥𝔦𝔰 𝔴𝔞𝔰 𝔱𝔥𝔢 𝔰𝔱𝔶𝔩𝔢 𝔥𝔢 𝔠𝔬𝔭𝔦𝔢𝔡, 𝔞𝔫𝔡 𝔟𝔩𝔞𝔠𝔨𝔩𝔢𝔱𝔱𝔢𝔯 𝔟𝔢𝔠𝔞𝔪𝔢 𝔱𝔥𝔢 𝔣𝔦𝔯𝔰𝔱 𝔢𝔳𝔢𝔯 𝔭𝔯𝔦𝔫𝔱 𝔱𝔶𝔭𝔢𝔣𝔞𝔠𝔢.

In the fifteenth and sixteenth centuries, typographers influenced by Roman lettering developed cleaner typefaces that were easier to read. As printed material became more common, but was still expensive to create, designers took to modifying letter forms to save space and become more efficient at communication.

Some of these early modern typefaces, such as Baskerville and Bodoni, are still part of standard font bundles on Mac and PC today.

Desktop publishing has made us all typographers now.

Most of us who write electronically have opinions on what fonts we like best, and even on fonts we hate or think are ridiculous.

Some people choose different fonts on their e-readers to reflect the style of book they are reading. Students agonise over the choice of font when submitting an important essay; and with good reason. Phil Renaud, now a graphic designer, wrote a paper in 2006 in which he explored why his grade point average had improved over the course of the year, given that he didn't particularly feel he was putting any more work into his studying. He *had* changed the typefaces he used in his essays. Breaking down the fifty-two essays he submitted:

- Those he wrote in Georgia had an average grade of A
- Those he wrote in Times New Roman had an average grade of A–
- Those he wrote in Trebuchet had an average grade of B–

As we read words, we consume type. As we buy, we use it to help us navigate our selections. What the experts believe about how typography works is not always shared by consumers, but there are some common rules we recognise, even if we can't always articulate them. WE KNOW THAT IN EMAILS AND TWEETS, THIS IS THE EQUIVALENT OF SHOUTING, EVEN WITHOUT EXCLAMATION MARKS. We understand that *italics* on one word in a sentence implies special emphasis *on* that word, *but that if a whole sentence or paragraph is written in italics, it implies speed of forward motion; we read it more quickly.*

Every time we choose a product to buy, type is helping to influence our decision.

Type as communication of language

The first job type has to do, and the surface level of the way we experience it, is that it has to be clear and legible, and able to communicate information. Different typefaces are better at this in different situations.

When we're first learning to read, we're taught with sans-serif, lower case fonts because this makes different letter shapes much easier to recognise.

The same principle holds for road signs and public transport, particularly useful for when conditions may impede visibility or people need to be able to read something from a distance.

CAPITALS, WHICH DON'T HAVE AS MUCH VARIATION IN TERMS OF LETTER SHAPE, MAY CARRY MORE SERIOUSNESS BUT ARE NOT AS EASILY LEGIBLE.

Whereas if you're reading a book or other long piece of text at close quarters, serif fonts seem to flow more cleanly than sans serif, for a smoother reading experience. On the subject of which, nothing is more irritating when reading a long piece of text than the constant changing of fonts. We become uncomfortable if more than two fonts are used in close conjunction.

So I'll stop doing it now.

In brand design, fonts have several different uses. We'll talk specifically about logotype in the next chapter. But packaging has to communicate so much more than simply the name of the manufacturer.

In beer, if we're buying a can or bottle, there's a lot of statutory information that has to go somewhere on the label: net liquid content, alcohol content, best before date, probably some health warnings, a barcode, and ingredients. Then there's optional detail that a brewer probably wants to include if there's any space left: beer style, tasting notes, hop varieties, details of awards won and contact information are all common. In total, there can be as many as 250 words on a beer can or bottle – about the same as a single, full, typeset page in a novel – and they all need to be clearly legible.

Given that a prospective purchaser isn't going to waste any time over information that is unclear, a good designer needs to be able to navigate and direct your eye to the bits that matter in an order that makes sense. Some messages need to be central while others are peripheral: when dealing with unfamiliar beers, drinkers often make decisions based on the beer style and ABV, so these elements need to catch the eye first. Health warnings are arguably featured more grudgingly: next time you pick up a beer can or bottle, try to read everything on the pack and note the order in which your eye is drawn to all the various bits of information, and the health warning will invariably be among the last few elements you spot.

It's also worth noting that as well as the typeface, the words themselves communicate a lot more than the simple information they contain. A brand can come across as friendly or aloof, corporate or renegade, original or clichéd based on the type of language it uses in pack copy. Innocent Smoothies created a revolution in packaging design when it launched with a typographical style and tone of voice that expanded on the promise of the brand name. All the pack copy and all the text on their web page is written in VAG Rounded, the 'learning to read' font displayed above. It's almost always lower case, and it speaks to you not in the confident, boastful tones most brands use, but in a modest, self-deprecating, *innocent* tone of voice, which was copied so widely it changed the way brands spoke to their consumers.

In beer, you can quickly tell which brewers have put some thought into their label copy and which are merely filling

This redrawn type fo
Fuller's plays heavily o
the brewery's heritag
and yet feels brilliantl
modern. This is th
skill of a type artist
On projects like thi
old typefaces will b
explored in archives an
redrawn, incorporatin
subtle modern hints lik
kerning on typefaces t
subliminally sugges
contemporaneit

space and assuming no one is going to read it anyway. 'Brewed using only the finest hops and barley' is used with the intention of signifying quality, but to someone who buys beer often, it's a signifier of laziness, a sentence you've read a thousand times. 'Uniquely triple-hopped' on a beer that has had bittering hops, aroma hops and dry hops added to it is marketing nonsense to anyone who knows that this is standard practice for many beer styles. As for 'premium', 'cold-filtered', 'easy drinking refreshment', and 'crafted', they're almost unbearable, and they are also about to be joined by words such as 'juicy', 'awesome' and 'crushable'. It's often in the detail where you can spot the brands that truly care about every aspect of their beer. If they truly do think it's different, and better than the rest, they'll tell you.

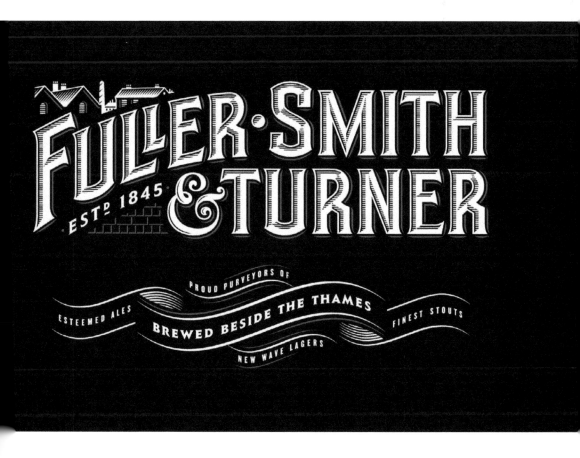

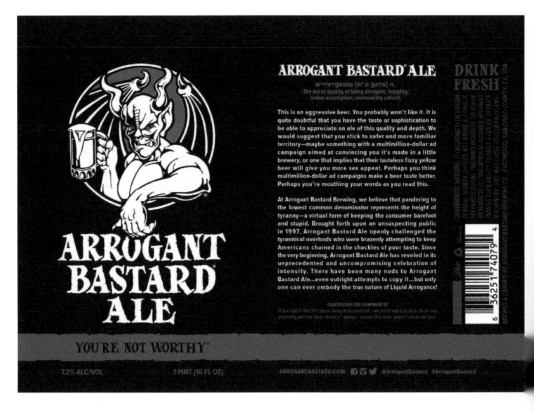

'This is an aggressive beer. You probably won't like it. It is quite doubtful that you have the taste or sophistication to be able to appreciate an ale of this quality and depth.'

With these words, California's Stone announced themselves as the 'antiInnocent', confrontational, challenging, and... well... arrogant bastards. It's a bold tone of voice, a tongue-in-cheek subversion of copywriting conventions and a demonstration of uncompromised passion for their beers. It has been copied countless times, sometimes ripped off wholesale, and has, like Innocent, influenced how an entire category communicates.

ST STEFANUS

St Stefanus is a Belgian abbey beer that was acquired by a global brewer and had its image smartened up. The new owners were particularly fascinated to learn that, as a bottle-conditioned beer, St Stefanus changes in character as it matures. This inspired a packaging approach that revels in the detail, inviting the drinker to pore over it and learn more about the beer as they are drinking it. Label graphics give an indication of how the taste evolves from three months to 18 months old (it'll carry on after that if you like, but food and drink labelling standards don't permit the brewer to say so.) To underline the importance of age, the date of bottling is added to every label, along with the signature of the head brewer.

Type as communication of emotion and personality

CRAFT BEER   **REAL ALE**   **CONTINENTAL LAGER**
Craft Beer   Real Ale   Continental Lager
Craft Beer   *Real Ale*   *Continental Lager*

Three beer styles, three typefaces, each of which has a distinct personality.
Which typeface feels right for which beer style?

Beneath the information being communicated literally, and what the tone of voice tells us about the personality of the brand, typefaces resonate with multiple layers of meaning by association, memory, and other responses that are almost impossible to explain.

It starts with the associations we have with fonts based on how and where we are used to seeing them. Their context gives them meaning, and that can be played with. Innocent chose a font we recognise from early childhood because it reminds us of when we, too, were innocent. Serif fonts in the early twentieth century were all about functionality. Sans serif fonts were then used to suggest something more modern and stylish. A flowing script suggests luxury, elegance and sophistication, while newspaper mastheads use heavy, gothic fonts to convey authority.

We can all tell the difference between a font that is old-fashioned and one that is futuristic, or a font that's artistic from one that is strictly functional. But on a deeper level, fonts also convey a whole range of different emotions. Sarah Hyndman runs type safaris, type tastings and other fun experiments that demonstrate how different fonts create and embody mood, emotion, story, noise, even deceit.

For example, which of these fonts is the happiest? Which font is faking its happiness?

Happy   HAPPY   Happy

Sarah puts these experiments together based on her intuition and understanding, and then tests them with large groups of people to see if she's right. By this method she can tell us, for example, that if three fonts walk into a pub, Helvetica, the 'everyman', will order a pint of lager, Times New Roman, 'the intellectual', will go for a decent white wine, while Comic Sans will get a round of shots in.

Typographer Alec Tear has worked on the lettering for beers including Fuller's and Budweiser. He prefers working with type rather than visuals because, contrary to the popular saying, he believes letters say more than pictures. 'There's so much history rooted in it,' he says. 'The associations in typography can take you to a place or tap into a feeling that visuals can't. If it's absolutely right, you didn't even notice it. Why does Budweiser look and feel American? You've probably seen it on an American bank note, or somewhere else you'll never be able to place.'

With this in mind, real ale pump clips seem to overwhelmingly favour block capitals in serif fonts. Big and chunky, they're clearly trying to create standout, but also suggest seriousness and stability. Emotionally, they seem po-faced, even repressed. This is often countered by putting the type on a curve rather than a straight line, which makes it seem more playful and energetic.

Mainstream lager fonts tend to split into two groups: some logo typefaces are old-fashioned and haughty, desperate to convince you of an authentic heritage, while others are neutral, sans-serif, everyman and relatable.

Craft beer, obviously, is a mixed bag, as it is in every other aspect of design. There's a lot of cool, functional, minimalist type to communicate modernity and sophistication, but also a lot of playfulness, with bespoke or hand-drawn fonts expressing exuberant personalities.

HEINEKEN

Freddy Heineken – grandson of founder Gerard Adriaan Heineken – was the man who transformed Heineken from a well-known brewer in the Netherlands into an international colossus. He was responsible for putting Heineken into green bottles, which massively helped the brand boost exports, particularly into the United States.

He is often also given the credit for a subtle change to the brand name typography. In 1951, Heineken changed its typeface from block capitals to lower case. But that's not all: look carefully at the 'e' letters in the name: they have been tilted slightly so they look like they're smiling, making the whole word subliminally look friendlier. Freddy also directed that the brand name be changed from 'Heineken's' to the slightly less stuffy 'Heineken'.

In truth, Heineken's smiling 'e' was being used in advertising in the 1930s, before Freddy joined the company. The identity of the real author of this neat typographical trick is lost in time. But Freddy recognised its value, and ensured it was used wherever the name 'Heineken' was written.

Eduardo Paolozzi was known in Scotland as the 'father of pop art'. The Edinburgh Beer Factory wanted to evoke the spirit of fun and creativity in Paolozzi's work, and had the font for the label hand-drawn to incorporate and reflect his style.

Solvay Society is a London brewer specialising in Belgian-style ales. The minimalist packaging makes clever use of type to suggest the character and personality of the beers: 'minimise', is small, lower case and friendly, befitting a table beer of 3.2%, whereas 'Tritium' looks and sounds strong, as befitting a 7.5% Tripel. 'Halmos', in the middle at 4.2%, is studiedly neutral.

Amity aims to revive
traditional beer styles
the modern craft beer
and their visual design
reflects this. The logo t
inspired by poster ads
the 1950s and 1960s, w
more modern san serif
for clear communicatio
The logo is tilted upwar
and forwards as a sign
progression and growth

Donzoko combines type
in an interesting way. T
brand is a playful take
gothic typeface that ev
continental brewing he
and heavy metal music
a perfect combination
beer. Individual beer na
in a neutral typeface b
placement of the type
it fun and irreverent.

...s & Gunn use bold, authoritative typefaces to evoke a sense of permanence and authenticity, which makes it hard to believe ...brand is less than twenty years old.

BUDWEISER

Rediscovering the genuine article

Beer brands have a particular problem with ageing, especially big ones, and there's no bigger beer brand in the Western world than Budweiser. Whereas brands in other markets can age gracefully (who thinks of Levi's as a Victorian brand, or Ray Ban as 1930s?) beer suffers from a sense of 'you don't drink what your dad drank'. This is now contracting, to not even drinking what your older brother drank. In the craft beer boom, brands can start to feel dated before they reach double figures.

Budweiser clearly felt defensive about craft beer, so much so that that company couldn't make up its mind how to respond. Owners Anheuser Busch made huge budget TV ads for Budweiser cruelly mocking people who drink craft beer, at the same time as going on a shopping spree to buy up craft brewers they liked the look of. 'Proud to be a macro beer', screamed poster ads, in language that macro beers and the people who drink them don't even use.

Budweiser proclaims itself the 'king of beers', and in design terms it had acquired all kinds of trinkets and baubles. There was embossing and detailing, texture and fake bling all over the brand. It looked fake. It looked cheap. And it looked like a brand that had forgotten who and what it was. It wanted to look modern and contemporary, deciding that this was best done with its bow-tie graphic, and it also wanted to play on tradition, which it did by playing up the

heritage in the script-like type. It couldn't do both simultaneously, and a move in either direction would alienate people on the other side.

Design agency jkr allegedly pointed all this out to Anheuser Busch by recreating a pretty close copy of the label design using fonts that come as standard with Microsoft Word. After a great deal of argument, they were given the go-ahead to overhaul the design.

They did so by going back to basics, scouring the archives for the soul of the brand. Every single element of the new design was drawn by hand by lettering artists. In total, seven different artists created fourteen separate unique typographical elements within the new design. All the fake

bling and special effects were stripped away. It was the typographical equivalent of one of those 'make under' reality shows where people addicted to extreme make-up and enhancement are given a more natural look.

This new look launched in 2016, and was celebrated throughout the design world as an absolute classic. The detail is less apparent to the casual observer, but even a design novice can feel that Bud now seems more authentic and true to itself than it did without even understanding why. That's why Bud enjoyed an extraordinary boost in sales after the new design was rolled out. Most of us may not be able to put our finger on what makes something feel right, but we can sense when it's there.

OTLEY 04
COLOMBO
ABV 4.0%

OTLEY 06
PORTER
ABV 6.6%

OTLEY 09
BLONDE
ABV 4.8%

OTLEY 10
OXYMORON
ABV 5.5%

OTLEY 11
MOTLEY BREW
ABV 7.5%

Welsh brewer Otley launched in 2005, before the craft beer revolution had really hit the UK. Their stark, minimalist use of the 'O' stood out against what was then a sea of traditional, homespun labelling, with the core range of beers being names 01, 02 and so on: an entire branding scheme making one letter work extraordinarily hard.

With various craft brewers now using one letter or digit as its focal point of brand design, we realised we'd seen one brand that has been doing this consistently for decades now. The big red 'T' of Tennent's is a design classic. In its native Scotland, it symbolises not just the brand, but beer itself.

The shape of the T is heavy and industrial, evocative of the docks and industry in Tennent's' native Glasgow. It works perfectly as an illuminated sign that shines from bar tops, and if you drive around Scotland, it hangs outside countless pubs, signalling from a distance, especially in poor weather or darkness, that this particular building is, in fact, a pub. It hasn't been updated in decades, because it doesn't need to be: it has a simplicity and directness that never seems to grow dated, and yet somehow remains distinct and ownable.

Design and language working together

Traditionally in beer or any other commercial graphic design, the back label is the poor cousin to the front. It's the place where all the statutory information goes, whereas the front label is for the name and logo, the glamour of the brand.

Some beers have subverted this trend to create highly original and distinctive designs. Pulling together the need to communicate information clearly and the power of type to convey personality, the traditional canvas of design can be subverted. What if you make the detail the focus of the brand identity rather than the messy stuff that gets shoved around the back?

This has been made much easier by the growth of cans. Instead of a front and back label, there's one cylindrical canvas. Every element – right down to the health warnings – has to be part of that same canvas. Some brands simply stick it all in a panel or strip, recreating the clutter of the traditional back label. Others incorporate it into the overall design scheme, making it a feature.

Making the detail the highlight, or integrating it into the design, says something powerful about the brand. It says, 'This is the stuff that's important to us. We care about the detail.' It's a great way of building authenticity and implying strong brewing credentials.

While – strictly speaking – it's not just about text, Good Chemistry is a great example of information design being the basis for the whole identity of the brand. The brewery took what they believe to be the five 'universal elements' of beer: hoppiness, maltiness, bitterness, sweetness and body. Each beer undergoes sensory analysis of these elements and that becomes the basis for its visual design.

Brew York's cans are a great combination of striking visuals and effective information design. It looks like as much care and attention has been put into conveying product details as has gone into making the main design bold and attractive.

Cloak & Dagger have gone one step further by dispensing with the information panel and incorporating essential text into the main design itself. While it could be argued that this makes the information more difficult to read, the way it's done actually draws the viewer in and makes you want to learn more.

BREW BY NUMBERS

Brew by Numbers doesn't just do good information design: the whole brand *is* good information design. It's been the DNA of the brewery from day one.

Every Brew by Numbers (usually abridged to BBNo) beer name is a four-digit catalogue number. The first two numbers denote the style of beer, with 01 being saison (saisons just happened to be the go-to craft beer style when the brewery was founded), 05 India Pale Ale, 19 Gose, and so on. The second two digits mark the specific release number within that style, so the first ever BBNo was 01|01. This approach inspired clear, informative labelling that looked modern and minimalist and at the same time like something from an ancient apothecary.

In 2018 the brand was refreshed to focus more on the first two numbers denoting beer style. Now when they produce beers away from their core range, they design custom numbers to convey something of the personality of each recipe.

CAMDEN TOWN

If it ain't broke... you know what? Maybe you can still fix it.

Don't you wish you'd thought of calling a brewery Camden Town? The North London district may now have turned into a theme park facsimile of itself, but globally, Camden – the place – is a brand in the same way that Brooklyn, Paris or Rio de Janeiro are brands: they're not just physical places. You could say that something is 'Parisian' and be referring to style or attitude and people would understand exactly what you meant by that.

So when Camden Town launched in 2010 the branding task was very straightforward: create a visual identity that evoked Camden: a set of values that just happened to chime

perfectly with the young, irreverent, energetic spirit of craft beer at the time.

It worked. The packaging and the attitude it represented helped make Camden one of the darlings of the UK craft beer movement (great beer played a part too.) So much so, that in 2015, after just five years in operation, Camden was bought by A-B InBev for £85 million.

Camden's beers are of excellent quality, but they're also more accessible than more eclectic and experimental craft brews. Putting aside the disappointment in craft beer circles about 'selling out', Camden was the perfect brand for a company with A-B InBev's marketing and

distribution muscle to introduce craft beer to a mass-market, mainstream audience.

As part of this, Camden undertook a refresh of its branding that aimed to keep its rebellious spirit intact while beefing up the various elements of the design to work harder in a raw commercial mainstream market.

The logo was simplified and made bolder, and the commitment to using strong, vibrant colours was kept. But all the heavy lifting in the new design, introduced in 2016, is done by typography.

The single word 'Camden' is made much bolder than the old 'Camden Town Brewery', and presented as a nameplate that's reminiscent of those on the canal boats around Camden's locks. This is balanced by the clean lozenge at the bottom of the label which makes it very clear what style of beer is in the bottle.

All of this is classic branding: a simplified design where each element works hard – there's nothing that doesn't need to be here – and it's all a lot more corporate and professional than the previous labels.

(cont.)

Then, within this safe, professional, and quite conventional framework, the name of each beer goes off in the opposite direction typographically. Each bit of type is joyously playful, steeped in popular culture, each with its own identity and personality. Only when you see these central names out of context, without the brand framework surrounding them, can you see how loud and rambunctious they are.

Altogether, the redesign somehow manages to be more mainstream, commercial and accessible, but also more Camden – the spirit of the place – at the same time. In design terms this doesn't feel like a brand that's sold out: it feels like a brand that's re-expressed its energy in a way more people will get.

‘probably the best
logo in the world’

5

Logos and Names

Yo, Logo!

The logo is the smart-bomb of brand design, a concentrated hit of meaning that works insanely hard when done well. A good logo is usually the centrepiece of effective branding, the resolution to the story the rest of the design or ad is telling.

When we see branding in that first split second, our eye takes in shape and colour before we read words. The power of the logo is totemic, to a degree that it has become the butt of the biggest and least funny joke in advertising and brand design. I can personally guarantee that every single person who has worked in these professions has experienced on at least one occasion feedback from their client after a presentation of new work, which goes along the lines of, 'We think it looks great. Just one tweak: could we make the logo bigger?'

And we as consumers care passionately about logos too. You may not think you do, and you probably never notice how much you do care ... until the logo is changed. When brands like Airbnb and Instagram modernised logos that had been around since they were small start-ups, fans took to social media to say how much they hated the new design, to the extent that it had ruined their day. Retailer Gap and football team Leeds United both announced new logos that created such hostile reactions among their fans that they were quickly forced to scrap them, consigning months of expensive design work to the bin.

We like logos so much because they become part of the fabric of our lives: common features in our fridges and store cupboards, or as icons on our phones and desktops.

A logo can consist of text, shapes or visuals, or a combination of all three. Where the logo includes text as opposed to running alongside separate text, that text will be highly stylised, perhaps the signature of the founder of the company (Disney, Kellogg's), a highly stylised typeface (Google, Coca Cola) or even a single letter (the 'Golden arches' of McDonald's). When the logo is just an image, it will usually be one that has been smoothed away and made instantly recognisable, again highly stylised, so that when you see it, you think of the company it represents rather than the object it supposedly is (the Nike tick, Shell, Penguin, the Starbucks mermaid.) When the logo is a name and an image together, we are seeing the thing visually represented at the same time as we are reading it, a double hit of communication that sears itself onto the memory.

Creating a logo is one of those tasks that is simple to pick up, yet very difficult to master. That's why leading design agencies are very happy to tell you how to do it yourself. The design should stand out. It needs to be simple, clear and legible. You should use colour, but also consider that the logo will occasionally appear in black and white. It should be scalable so that it can look impressive on a huge banner, but also legible at the bottom of a tiny newspaper ad.

Follow these rules and anyone with a screen and a mouse can create a logo that – on the surface at least – looks like it has been done professionally. That's why hundreds of businesses around the world all have near-identical logos following the basic design that has become known in design circles as 'the hipster X' logo. Successful logos should not be generic and interchangeable. They should ideally express the personality of the brand and the story behind it. And that's why those design agencies seemingly giving away their secrets eventually end up with more clients by doing so.

The oldest logos in beer are simple shapes: the red hand of Allsopp's and the Bass red triangle were recognised around the world, in the same way as Budweiser's red bow tie is today. Shields as logos are ubiquitous as are ovals and ellipses, visuals that evoke the traditional 'racetrack' beer label but become more stylised and abstract as redesign follows redesign.

On starting this book, we couldn't think of many modern craft beer logos. The very idea of the logo feels a little too 'old school' for craft. But on closer examination, the logo is in rude health. Apart from giving a sense of gravity and permanence to new breweries, logos are being used in different ways: they are perfect as badges, and as stickers that fans can plaster on bags, laptops and smartphone cases. Reinvented and repurposed, the logo is bigger than ever.

BEER LOGOS

The agencies that create successful logos are paid a lot of money, so they're very keen to demonstrate the enormous power of logos in identifying brands. A popular way of doing this – which is now as popular in pub quizzes as it is in branding agency pitch presentations – is to 'de-brand' well-known logos to see if people can still name the brand. The point being, of course you can. Here are six de-branded beer logos. Can you name all six brands?

THE HIPSTER 'X' LOGO

The letter 'X' is mystical and powerful: it can bar the way, cross things out, suggest something is forbidden. Or it can tie things together, denote strength and potency, be a kiss, or just a mark of identification. It also divides a surface handily into four fields, into which four small images or letters can be deployed to create an instant logo. The first instance of this was the letters H-C and N-Y being used as a logo for the New York hardcore music scene in the early 1980s. All of this feeds into making the X-based logo so ubiquitous that it has become known within the design industry as 'the hipster X', appearing on literally thousands of coffee shops, barbers, bike shops and craft breweries around the world. (Images sourced from the 'Your logo is not hardcore' Tumblr.)

THE CRAFTING OF A GOOD LOGO

Type 'Craft beer logos' into a Google image search and most of the hits are for generic, off-the-shelf logos you can buy from designers, a dozen at a time, all completely interchangeable and forgettable. A successful logo differentiates. Those featured here each tell you something about the personality of the brewer rather than simply saying, 'This is beer'.

six°north

Howling Hops

Wander Beyond

Gun Brewery

Good Things Brewing

Brass Castle

McColl's Brewery

Mourne Mountains

North Brewing

Orbit

Round Corner

London Beer Factory

BROOKLYN

Owning the whole borough

Google any variation on 'top ten logos' and among them will be the I♥NY logo created by designer Milton Glaser for the city of New York in 1977. It made Glaser one of the most famous designers in the world, and he was profiled by publications such as *Time* magazine and the *New York Times*. He was so famous that when Brooklyn co-founder Steve Hindy phoned and asked to speak to him, the receptionist responded 'Do you know who Milton Glaser is? He doesn't just talk to *anyone*,' and refused to put him through.

This made Hindy – a former news reporter – more determined than ever. He phoned the same receptionist back every day, until she realised he wasn't going to give up, and finally put Glaser on the line. When Hindy explained that he was hoping to revive Brooklyn's once great brewing heritage, Glaser replied, 'That sounds like fun. Come in and see me.'

By this time, Milton Glaser was only working on projects that interested him personally. Unlike the other big design agencies Hindy visited, Glaser said he – the boss of the company – would be working on the project himself and would be Hindy's main point of contact. He also agreed to do the work in return for a small stake in the business, plus expenses.

Hindy's plan had been to launch a beer called Brooklyn Eagle Lager. Glaser dissuaded him from the eagle part, pointing out that Budweiser already used an eagle, and saying, 'Why sell a bird when you've got the whole borough?'

Hindy went away imagining depictions of the iconic Brooklyn Bridge, maybe some reference to the Dodgers. When he came bac and got a white 'B' on a green background, he was initially underwhelmed. 'Don't say a word,' said Glaser. 'Take this home and show it to your wife. Put it on the counter in your kitchen and live with it for a while.'

Eventually, the simple brilliance of the design sunk in. The cursive, flowing 'B' did,

fact, evoke the Brooklyn Dodgers, as well
s the creative flair of the entire borough.
somehow felt like it had been a fixture of
rooklyn for years, to the extent that some
eople believed Hindy and his business partner,
om Potter, were reviving an old institution
ather than creating something new.

Hindy and Potter immediately added the
logo to their business plan and it served as a
kind of validation of the business in the eyes
of potential investors. It has since gone on
to be not just one of the most recognisable,
iconic logos in beer, but a symbol of Brooklyn's
cultural and commercial renaissance.

The couple who set up Neptune previously ran an aquatics business, so water provides the story theme running through the range. The logo is the basis of the entire brand design, a bold statement that aims for strong recognition in a crowded line-up and a guarantee of quality.

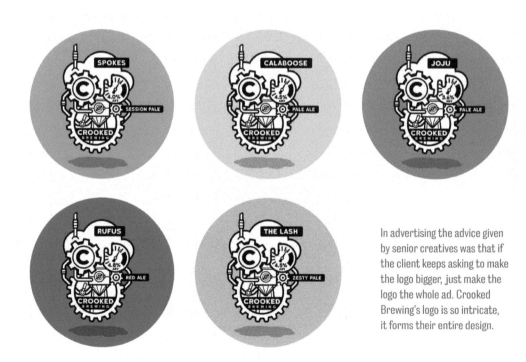

In advertising the advice given by senior creatives was that if the client keeps asking to make the logo bigger, just make the logo the whole ad. Crooked Brewing's logo is so intricate, it forms their entire design.

What's in a name?

Once upon a time, beer names were as simple as you could get. If Mr Smith made a beer, then his beer would be called Smith's Beer. If Mr Smith made a range of beers, they would be called Smith's Pale Ale, Smith's Mild, Smith's Bitter and so on. If Mr Smith had two sons and they fell out and became rival brewers, their beers might be called John Smith's and Samuel Smith's. The name of the beer was a simple indication of ownership, a credit to the founder of the brewery, whether they were called Guinness, Heineken, Bass, Worthington, Coors, Marston, Tennent, Foster, Tetley or Fuller.

The next most obvious naming strategy was place names: the town, city, district or street the brewery was founded in was used to give a sense of ownership of the place as well as a sense of identity (Sussex Best, Barnsley Bitter.)

As branding grew more common in the twentieth century, some of those breweries looked to build brands that stood alone. Early individual beer names could be expressions of quality of superiority (Marston's Pedigree, London Pride, Master Brew) and developed along various lines such as indicators of strength (6X, Old Peculier, Tanglefoot) or descriptions of the beer (Harvest Pale, Daleside Blonde, Brain's Dark). As guest ales became more common, seasonal themes such as Winter Warmer, Autumn Red or Rocking Rudolph were also easily done.

These all worked fine in pubs, and a check of any mainstream beer list shows that, between them, these strategies are still responsible for most beer names.

But as the majority of the beer we drink has shifted from the on-trade to the off-trade, beer has started having to compete like any other product commonly referred to as a fast-moving consumer good (FMCG). As a result, we've seen beer names diversify in scope from being simple descriptions, or claims of ownership or quality, into a language that's far more creative, with good and bad results.

Naming a new product that's intended to be permanent is a slow and painstaking process. The convention is to list as many candidates as possible, words that describe the product, what it does or how it makes you feel, and then test them, research them, check them against records, and gradually whittle them down over time.

In the early twentieth century it became common to make up words that sounded right, or distinctive. These might be acronyms (Tesco, OMO) or abbreviations (Daz), but sometimes they were totally made-up words that had no meaning other than that the brand gave to them: or so the marketers believed. Words that are meaningless in one language can be very meaningful in another. Beer has been relatively unscathed in this respect because it remains more localised than other products, but car manufacturers seem to have an unfortunate tendency to open themselves to ridicule. Spanish seems to be particularly problematic: Mazda launched their Laputa without realising this translated as 'the whore'; Nova, a model name used by both Chevrolet and Lada, translates as 'doesn't work'; while Lamborghini's two-million-dollar Reventón means 'blow-out' or 'flat tyre'.

According to the rules of beer branding, the name of a product has to be something people feel comfortable saying at the bar. For starters, they at least need to be able to pronounce it without fear of being laughed at for getting it wrong. The exception to this are the novelty names given to seasonal beers: a surprisingly large number of people still find it hilarious to ask for an Old Growler, a Dizzy Blonde or a bit of Slap & Tickle.

Like so much else, craft beer has challenged the conventions around beer names. Product descriptors are louder and more sensationalised, with lots of juice, fruit, haze and hops, with potency and darkness also featuring strongly. Nods to popular culture are far more common, which has given the pun a new lease of life with beers such as Born to be Mild, Joined at the Hop and Rhubarbra Streisand cropping up at festivals around the country.

With so many new beers being launched, the problem with coming up with a snappy, product-related name is that the idea you just had, that brilliant pun that made everyone in the room laugh, has probably been used already. I just googled 'Hoptimus Prime' (hilarious!) and found five different beers produced by five different breweries on the first page of results. These days, when a brewer comes up with a great 'new' name for a beer, they should firstly, if they're sensible, check a website such as Untappd to see if it's already been taken.

The fact that it probably has been taken encourages brewers to become more creative in their ideas for naming: names become longer, each word reducing the probability that it's already been used. They become less directly beer focused, and therefore less obvious. They may tell a story about the brewers, their friends, their families or their pets: something the consumer doesn't need to know or understand in order to enjoy the way the words run together, but which creates an undercurrent of meaning nevertheless.

An additional advantage to this approach rests on the fact that in craft beer bars with ten, twenty or thirty taps, visual branding is no longer practical. There isn't enough space for individual fonts on the bar, so the beers are listed by name and style on a chalkboard or beer menu. There are no visual cues, just a name, ABV and price, and if there's space, a notation of style. In this situation, random, mysterious, evocative or funny names are all a brewer has in their struggle to stand out and be distinctive.

When your brewery is named after the colour Robin Hood was reputed to have worn, the names of individual beers pretty much write themselves. Each beer in the core range reminds us of another character from the legend.

Look closely, and Red Willow's weeping willow logo is made up of Rs and Ws ('Red' and 'Willow' are the middle names of the children of brewery founders Toby and Caroline McKenzie.) The clean, consistent house style is further strengthened by the naming scheme of the beers: each name ends in the -less suffix.

Designer Leigh Pierce says the names of Cloak & Dagger beers are abstract and not descriptive of the beers themselves. Often our names rhyme – this comes from my hip-hop background and experience of writing rap lyrics,' he says. 'I enjoy the syllabic sound the names make: Komodo Bozo, Galactic Catnip, Gigantic Antics, Routes to Pluto.'

Ve are modernist,' say And nion in their blurb. 'The basic rinciples of modernism re purity, rationality and mplicity and the honest xpression of the nature of aterial and their quality.' nd what could be simpler d more honest than ggesting which day of the eek is right for each beer?

GUINNESS

The national symbol that rediscovered cra

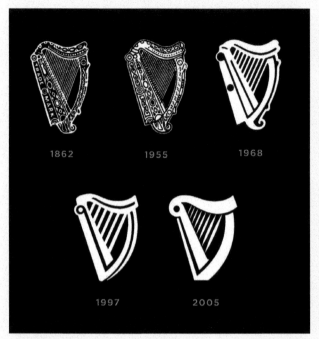

1862   1955   1968

1997   2005

Brian Boru was High King of Ireland from 1002 to 1014, and has been credited as a key figure in uniting the country. He's a legendary figure in Irish history, father of the O'Brien surname, and was also a keen harp player. The Trinity Harp, on display in Trinity College in Dublin, is almost certainly not Brian Boru's personal instrument, but it's such a great story it seems a shame to disbelieve it. Either way, this medieval harp has become a symbol that says 'Ireland' wherever it appears around the world.

It was the obvious symbol for Guinness to use as its logo to identify the brand when it began focusing on exporting beer, and had been in use since 1862. It was registered

as a trade mark in 1876, the same years as Bass. When the Irish government wanted to adopt the harp as Ireland's national symbol in 1922, they had to switch the harp around so as not to infringe Guinness's trade mark: the sound box – the thick, upright part – was inverted from the left to the right.

As discussed above, when real-world objects become logos, there's a tendency for their representation to become more stylised and symbolic. The first Guinness harp was very detailed, with some elements that didn't really reproduce well when printed. Between 1862 and 2005, the logo harp was simplified and smoothed away, until it became a flat, two-dimensional abstract representation

perhaps the serifs
could be cut short

of a harp – recognisable, but not real.
It was certainly iconic, but it had lost
some of its soul', says Graham Shearsby,
creative director of Design Bridge,
who were appointed to do a redesign.
It looked a little lonely. And at the time,
craft beer was really taking off.
Handcrafted values were important.
We wanted to make the harp sing again.'

Design had become increasingly
computerised. Design Bridge decided to
bring it back to the real world, and did so
in the most literal way imaginable. They
made models and mock-ups of the harp,
working closely with London-based harp-
makers Niebisch and Tree. This gave the

designers a real understanding of the
harp's shape and form, its curves and
shadows. They then employed renowned
illustrator Gerry Barney – who drew a
previous version of the harp in 1968 – to
draw the final harp based on the various
sketches and models. Only when the entire
thing was finished was it finally digitised.

The new design hit the shelves in late
2016 – or at least, it hit some shelves. At the
time of writing, a picture search of Guinness
reveals that some shops and supermarkets
are still using outdated visuals of the old
design. This is odd: the new harp brings the
brand a sense of warmth and genuine craft,
and would surely sell more Guinness.

Comedian Stewart Lee once did a routine about craft beers with strange names like 'Gandalf's Memory Stick'. It doesn't matter how hard even the best comedians in the world try to satirize this trend, real craft beer names will always be funnier and weirder.

'where do you
want to go today?'

6

Visual Identity

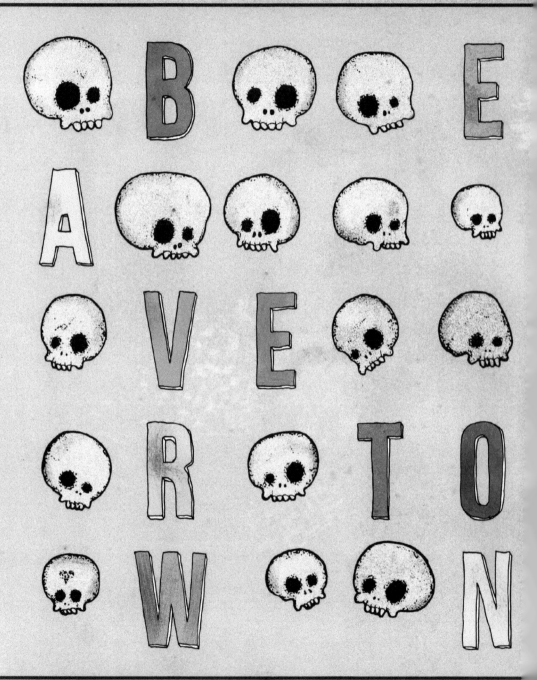

BEAVERTOWN'S
MAGNIFICENT SKULPHABET

A LEARNING TOOL FOR TOOLS OF ALL AGE

Telling the story in pictures

The modern rules of branding are fixed and well-known, having been built on the back of decades of experience, countless hours of market research, thousands of failures, and billions of dollars in profits for those who get it right. These rules include commandments such as:

- Be clear and iconic in your design
- Have a good idea of what your brand is all about and make sure it sits behind everything you do
- Tell a good story
- Be consistent across every point at which people come into contact with your brand
- Try not to look like everybody else

When a brand gets all these things right, and grows to become worth millions or even billions as a result, the people working it become very nervous about changing anything or deviating from any of these rules. A slight tweak to the colour palate, a smoothing of the kerning of a typeface, is a process that can take years, cost hundreds of thousands, and then be unveiled as a revolutionary move.

This is why visual elements of design are less important in big brands than logos or typefaces. Visuals contain so much information they can date quickly, or tie a brand down too specifically in once place. Where visuals form part of the identity of a large brand, they're usually smoothed down and simplified as much as possible.

Visual elements such as illustration, painting, cartoons, patterns or characters are used far more often across ranges

of beers than in stand-alone products, and are most common for seasonal and limited-edition beers. The main requirement for design is different here. For a range, visuals can create some variety and individuality in design schemes in concert with other elements that reinforce that the beers are all part of the same family. For limited-edition and seasonal beers, the design doesn't necessarily need to build a brand that's going to last forever. Rather, it needs to stand out on the bar or bottle shop and prompt a reaction of 'Ooh, I haven't seen that before.'

The element of design best practice that visually-led ranges have in common with stand-alone text and logo-driven beers is that they are still expected to tell a good story. The subject matter of the illustration might be a local legend, an evocation of place or people, a story about how the beer is made or what's in it, or even a gag or joke to give you a momentary smile.

The style of the design also allows a brewer to tell you pretty clearly who they are: are they homespun and traditional, with a folksy, rootsy, or even amateurish illustration style? Or are they cool and modern, making use of textured visuals created by desktop design apps?

Like a good stamp collection, pull a compendium of good beer brand design together and it tells you stories of history, community and the world around you as well as brewing.

Not everybody has to look colourful and counter-cultural. Newbarns is a celebrated new brewery that evokes traditional Belgian and German beer design cues. The branding was actually inspired by an old box of beer mats dating from the 1940s to the 1980s which was discovered at an auction.

But as with every other aspect of beer design, the rules are now changing, and sometimes – for better or worse – being thrown out of the window altogether.

Fractured narratives

Over the last twenty years the visual design of beer has become more innovative as the market has become more crowded. Until the mid-2010s there were clear trends that followed one after the other. Real ale pump clips were hand-drawn or painted illustrations, often featuring natural landscapes, seasonal scenes, visual gags or local stories. Photography was hardly ever used, because when it was it looked weird and wrong, like a novelty beer from a joke brewery.

After BrewDog shook up the beer market, craft beer exploded in a riot of disruptive, anti-establishment imagery. Beavertown changed the agenda again with its playful mash-up of kitsch pop-cultural imagery, friendlier than BrewDog, yet still somehow threatening, playful, nostalgic and revolutionary, all at the same time. Then Cloudwater reinvented the beer label as the frame for a piece of abstract art.

Northern Monk is at the heart of Britain's craft brewing scene, with varied, bold and eye-catching packaging that nevertheless keeps to the rules of effective commercial branding. The central monk acts like a guardian and guarantor of creativity and character.

Each time, the pioneering brands were breaking some of those supposedly intractable rules of what made brand design work. And each time, like a cluster of eight-year-olds playing football, when the innovators moved into empty space, the pack slavishly followed, keeping pace with their every move.

Since around 2015, all bets are off. The hottest trends in visual design have become almost impossible to keep track of, because they're firing off in all directions, including backwards, all at once. Any sense of norms is fragmenting. The only convention is the breaking of convention itself.

The stories that brands were telling through their visual design became more oblique. Instead of saying something about the beer itself or the people who made it or the place it came from, label design art started to convey a mood or an aesthetic. Particularly after the reinvention of cans, beer design started to work in the way classic vinyl album covers had, filling a gap that had been created by music moving to

Gipsy Hill creates a brand personality for its core range in the most literal way imaginable: each beer features a member of the Gipsy Hill team or one of their industry friends, immortalised by artist Marcus Reed.

an online streaming format. These were designs that needed to be stared at and analysed, theorised over, by people who would later insist they were into the beer before anyone else, and always preferred the brewery's earlier stuff.

The most abstract and mysterious designs were initially reserved for special releases. Core branding still had to work hard to build an identity and tell a story in the long term, whereas the beer can as a work of abstract art actually *hid* the brand, suggesting that this can wouldn't be around for long. It also hinted that the beer was experimental, a break from how this brewer usually did things: if the design was this bold, with graphics exploding off every inch of the can and few if any of the normal brand design elements present to clutter things up, then the beer was probably similarly out-there too.

The lack of permanence of these beers was subtly enhanced by the use of pressure-sensitive labelling: instead of printing the design directly onto the can, it was printed on adhesive paper which the patient drinker might even be able to peel off in one piece. This worked brilliantly to help establish the reputation of hazy New England IPAs as beers that had to be drunk within a few weeks of being brewed, and might not return in exactly the same way ever again because of variations in the hop supply, the attention deficit disorder of the brewer, or the endless quest for novelty of the drinker. Grab it while you can: it may not be here tomorrow and chances are you wouldn't want it if it was.

Used for collaboration brews, this approach to design solved the problem of co-branding: a unique one-off design with no relation to either brewery's core branding can carry two logos as easily as one, with all brewers involved sharing equal status.

If these beers turn out to be great, the design helps make them collectable and give them bragging rights on social media. It gets the brewer featured in not just the beer trade press, but design magazines too. If the beer turns out to be rubbish, that's OK because its presence is transient and it didn't have any lasting effect on the parent brand.

The end of storytelling?

'This is awesome! Wait, who made this again?'

This is a quote from America brand design agency CODO in their annual summary of trends in beer brand design. It's a response to the trend of the convention-busting approach towards limited brands increasingly creeping into the design of beers that are supposedly core and permanent: self-adhesive labels featuring oblique, mysterious branding seem to be becoming common for any craft beer.

If it works to build hype and attention around special releases, then maybe it will do the same for core releases. But there are two sides to this: if the design of the beer doesn't shout about who brewed it, how are drinkers going to remember the beers they loved? If everybody is doing wildly different abstract visual design work, are you only as good as the latest cool artist you feature on your can?

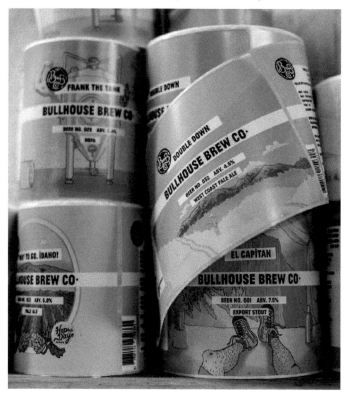

Self-adhesive labels work practically in making can design for short runs and limited editions much more practical and affordable. But by symbolising that, they also send a coded message that this is a beer that may be tricky to get hold of and may not be around for too long.

What happens when a rival brewer signs a cooler artist? And if you're changing design every few months, what happens when you eventually run out of new artists to work with?

There are different views among seasoned commercial designers about the extent to which this is a problem waiting to blow up in the face of the enterprising, visually-led brewer. Is storytelling by beer brands becoming less important? Or just changing in nature?

It's arguable that these dramatic shifts in beer design are not just driven by an endless search for novelty and instagram-mability; although that's certainly part of it. Beer brands generally seek to reassure prospective drinkers that they are of superior quality, more 'premium' than what you might have been drinking before. My friend Sarah Hyndman, the typographer, suggested that the way 'premiumness' is expressed has changed. 'A few years ago it was all about the bling,' she argues. 'Now, it's all about authenticity and experience and being who you are.'

This is an interesting insight when you compare how this vague notion of 'premium' is executed in traditional main-stream beer design compared to modern craft. Mainstream lager brands love a bit of bling: their labels are encrusted in gold and silver. Using Sarah's analysis, the medals that many of these labels carry, centred just below the main logo, suddenly look like the medallions of the 1970s/1980s self-styled 'ladies' man'. These days medallion man is an anachronism on the dating scene, at best seen as a figure of fun. What works now (so I'm told) is being honest, open and genuine.

This is difficult to achieve – both in marketing and dating (which in a weird way, is a form of marketing) – when you're trying to balance it with putting the best version of yourself forward and convince someone that you really are the one they want to be with. And maybe the truth is, there still is a little bit of artifice involved. Before we leave the dating analogy behind, it's worth noting that beer – for so long a product associated with masculinity – is suddenly so much more relatable to women in its new, abstract, more artistic packaging.

Brands have been shouting in our faces for too long. Starbursts and primary colours on packaging, shouting voices in TV ads, web pages that are genuinely difficult to read because of pop-up ads that spring to life when you roll over them, and videos that you never wanted to see playing in the corners of pages: all these create a continual sense of being assaulted – or at least harassed – whenever we engage with the outside world.

In such a noisy environment, the strong and silent type suddenly looks more interesting. A well-executed premium beer brand allows you to come to it rather than chasing you down the street. The sense that you have discovered it makes it feel more special, and makes you feel cleverer.

The best contemporary beer branding still tells stories about itself, but it does so in a more genuine and more laid-back way. The details might be encoded. Some of the meaning may even be private, the people behind the brewery telling stories to themselves, so you can kind of 'hear' the story being told without quite being able to make sense of it, which adds an air of mystique, a desire to know more. This in itself isn't new: effective marketing has long benefited by asking the consumer to do a bit of the work instead of spoon-feeding them, getting their involvement and engagement by asking them to close the circle.

As consumers or drinkers, we feel an extra bit of satisfaction when we engage in this way: we know something other people don't. We've figured it out. Returning to the analogy with music, it's like we have a white-label version of a record before anyone else, seeing something and hearing something they can't. Relationships between buyer and seller forged in this way are far deeper than when someone simply feels they've been beaten over the head until they've handed over their money.

The problem with this approach is if you're one of the people who doesn't get all the hidden cues and clues. If oblique cultural references pass you by, or if you simply don't get what's meant to be going on, you can feel deliberately excluded by the brand in question, like they're saying you're just not hip enough to come in.

There's also the very real probability that, rather than meaning being hidden, coded or private, there's simply no meaning there at all.

'I worry that a lot of it is just design masturbation rather than brand-building,' says Silas Amos. Silas and I worked together on Stella Artois between 1997 and 2000. Since then, he's also helped create the visual design for brands such as Guinness and Budweiser, but he gets really excited by what he's seen brewers such as Beavertown and Camden Town do. 'Some of the rules of design are there for a reason,' he continues. 'If you've got a meaningless pattern with loads of colour clash, what are we as consumers meant to be thinking? Everything on a piece of design should be there for a reason. If there is no reason, it's just wallpaper. If it doesn't evoke a feeling or emotional response, it's not working. It says this beer is modern and contemporary, but so are all the other beers next to it. Beyond that, it's nothing.'

Modern beer design may be radically different from the fusty images on real ale pump clips or the sober bling of global lager brands, but it still needs to do the same job. It needs to make a promise, tell a story, and forge a relationship with the person thinking of buying a beer. Some design agencies specialising in craft beer are now seeing more breweries coming to them requesting rebrands as they have grown and consolidated rather than new breweries looking for their first visual identity. Brewers who have pushed the limits and broken all the rules of commercial brand design are finding that re-establishing those rules is the latest way to break contemporary design conventions.

There's a lot of lovely art and design out there on beer cans and bottles just now, more than ever before. This part of the book celebrates the stuff that actually says something about the beer, the place it is made, and the people who make it.

Pomona Island reacted against the maximalist trend in craft beer design by going for simple, impactful block colours, and creating interest with a combination of cute illustrations and an often-hilarious naming scheme. 'The main objective of good can design is to show the customer you've thought about it and you give a shit,' says Pomona Island's Nick Greenhalgh.

The natural world

Beer has always been about escape. A pint is a reward at the end of a hard day, a temporary respite from the bustle of modern life. Sometimes a beer will depict the countryside as a way of showing where it's from. Other times, it does so in a way that's more escapist, offering you a vision of a blissful place that echoes the promise of the pint itself to transport you.

Beer is also, let us not forget, a natural product. Too often, large, mainstream beer brands conjure up images of big factories churning out a product that's wrapped in chrome and steel throughout its entire process, then packaged in aluminium. Even before this, Victorian breweries tended to be tall, redbrick buildings spouting smoke and steam, catering primarily for populations working in factories, mines and mills. It pays to remind drinkers of the rolling fields of barley where beer is born, the magical lanes of hops hanging heavy on the bine, and the clear spring water that unites them in beer.

More recently, one of the main sources of craft beer's appeal is that people working in open-plan offices and pointless, soul-destroying jobs can live vicariously through the achievements of others. The beers we choose at the end of the day are symbolic acts where we pledge affinity to a more straightforward, meaningful and fulfilled life, silently rebelling against the system that holds us in place. Craft brands have played with representations of the countryside, making it more fantastical or dreamlike.

fred Wainright's beautifully
ind-drawn guidebooks are a fixture of
e Lake District, so it makes perfect
inse for the beer named in his honour
evoke his unique illustrative style.

Sierra Nevada started brewing in 1978. Founder Ken Grossman ran a home brew shop before going into brewing full time, as part of what he called a 'homesteading' lifestyle that involved a high degree of self-sufficiency. California in the 1970s was a place where the counter-cultural ideals of the hippie era were still popular, and it's no surprise that this is where modern craft beer began.

The painting of the Sierra Nevada mountains conjures up the sense of escape from the norm that early craft beer promised. It's not just the focus of the picture; it's the way it's been painted: the fact that it's done in a style that suggests a hobbyist painter rather than a professional. The homespun feel is the antithesis of slick corporate presentation and screams craft. In the early days of the American craft beer revolution, this was an important means of differentiation from the mainstream.

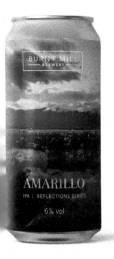

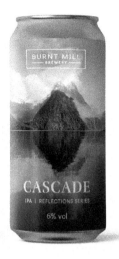

AMARILLO
IPA | REFLECTIONS SERIES
6% vol

BITTER LAKE
PALE ALE
5.5% ABV

CASCADE
IPA | REFLECTIONS SERIES
6% vol

FOUR RIVERS
PALE ALE
4.6% ABV

This artwork was originally inspired by the surroundings of Burnt Mill's farm in rural Suffolk. As the brewery's range broadened, the labels evolved to represent nature and landscape more generally, with a variety of different approaches and techniques.

Adnams launched Native Britten to mark the centenary of the centenary of Suffolk-born Benjamin Britten, who often drew inspiration from the Suffolk landscape. The designs are based on the land, sea and marshlands and are familiar to both composer and brewery.

The town of Cromarty sits on the Black Isle, a peninsula north of Inverness in the north-east of Scotland. The illustration style of natural scenes depicts an environment that is perilous as well as beautiful.

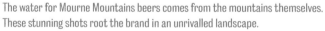

The water for Mourne Mountains beers comes from the mountains themselves. These stunning shots root the brand in an unrivalled landscape.

Church, state
and authority

Beer, like bread, has for most of human history been a necessity in the countries where it's drunk. As both an important source of nutrients – 'liquid bread' – and a mind-altering intoxicant, it has always therefore been tightly regulated and controlled.

This works in more ways than one: firstly, in many ancient legends, beer was a gift from the gods. In the Middle Ages, before we knew what yeast was, brewers referred to it as 'godisgoode' – a literal, everyday miracle. Secondly, from the Middle Ages onwards the Church was associated with brewing the best beer, both for internal use in monasteries and for guests and pilgrims. And thirdly, as well as regulating consumption of beer and taxing the proceeds of selling it, Church and State also introduced rules to ensure the quality of beer and reassure thirsty drinkers they were getting good beer in the right measures.

All of these aspects give Church, Crown and State a big role in the design of beer over the ages. They might not be so important now, but even commercial brewers who have never had any direct connection with these institutions will adopt some of the visual language of those brewers who have: coats of arms, badges and seals of approval, images of monasteries, churches or stained glass, crowns, crests and an awful lot of gold.

This all provided the standard in visual design against which craft beer would ultimately rebel. But in some places, in an uncertain world, these symbols of continuity and tradition can still reassure us.

ORVAL

Orval is one of the six great Belgian Trappist brands, and remains one of those beers that people who go on a journey of exploration through the exciting world of craft beer ultimately end up coming back home to. Bottle-conditioned, it's an intriguing beer that develops over time, to the extent that in the best Belgian beer bars 'out of date' bottles will sell at a premium compared to the fresh stuff.

The shape of the bottle and the small, classy label suggest mystery and class: this beer is unlike any other. The typeface clearly suggests a religious connection. The key visual of the brand, behind the text on the label, shows a fish with a ring in its mouth. According to legend, the widowed Countess Mathilda of Tuscany accidentally dropped her wedding ring in a spring. Distraught, she prayed for its return, and a trout emerged from the spring with the ring in its mouth. 'Truly this place is a *Val d'Or* [Golden Valley]', she exclaimed, and duly financed the building of an abbey on the spot.

The fabled spring still feeds the brewery at the Abbaye Notre-Dame d'Orval, and the legend gives a centuries-old legacy to a beer that was first brewed in 1931.

Beers that have their heritage in abbeys and monasteries unfailingly evoke this in their packaging, particularly the lettering and elements from coats of arms. They may not be the most exciting visually but they are timeless and evoke a guarantee of superior quality.

WILD BEER CO

When it launched in 2012, Bristol's Wild Beer Co had that rarest of qualities: a new, original story that was different from what everyone else was talking about. Each beer was brewed with a wild fifth ingredient on top of beer's usual four – be that an alternative fermentation, unorthodox yeast, seasonally foraged ingredient or esoteric and exotic produce.

From the very beginning, the branding needed to reflect that this was a brewery different from the others. Taking inspiration from the countryside around the dairy farm where the brewery began, the stag represents the combination of wildness and elegance the brewers seek to capture in the beers. These illustrations show how the logo evolved from being two rutting stags to something more ambiguous.

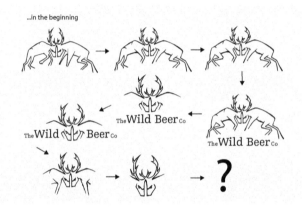

The animal kingdom

Animals are one of the most enduring and consistent visual themes in beer, cutting across all categories, from the most traditional old beers to modern craft. Sometimes an animal might be depicted because it relates directly to the brewing process or beer style: for example, goats are synonymous with German bock beers. Animals may be mythical creatures evoking some kind of symbolism from legend, such as dragons or great sea monsters signifying strength and power. More often, in rural areas animals that are notable to the local area tie the beer to its location. They might evoke character traits, the personality of the brewery itself or the people behind it: birds signify freedom, wolves or bears power, and monkeys are currently popular because they're a bit daft, especially in a space suit or lounging in a hammock with drink in hand. And then there are dogs. Dogs are loyal, happy and fun, our best friends, and therefore temperamentally suited to a life around beer in a way some other animals we could mention simply are not. A good pub has to have a dog lying in front of a fire or gazing at you longingly as it tries to hypnotise you into sharing your pub lunch. BrewDog was built around Bracken, an adorable mutt who was referred to as the founder and commander-in-chief of the brewery until he passed away in 2012. Dogs, monkeys and goats then: the poster animals of classic beer design.

BADGERCAN
SINGLE HOP MOSAIC
IPA 5.6% ABV

NO HEROES
BEER DOING GOOD

BISONCAN
HAZELNUT CHOCOLATE
PORTER 5.2% ABV

NO HEROES
BEER DOING GOOD

EAGLECAN
AMERICAN RED ALE
5% ABV

NO HEROES
BEER DOING GOOD

OCTOCAN
HAZY PALE ALE 4.5% ABV

NO HEROES
BEER DOING GOOD

No Heroes care as much about the environment as they do about their beer, so animals form the basis of their branding. The monochrome illustration style, inspired by Edwardian lithographs of inventions, is highly distinctive in a market dominated by bold colour.

ORANGUCAN
TROPICAL IPA 4.0% ABV

NO HEROES
BEER DOING GOOD

OTTERCAN
NEPA 4.7% ABV

NO HEROES
BEER DOING GOOD

PUFFINCAN
KVEIK IPA 6.5% ABV

NO HEROES
BEER DOING GOOD

SPIDERCAN
PILSNER 5% ABV

NO HEROES
BEER DOING GOOD

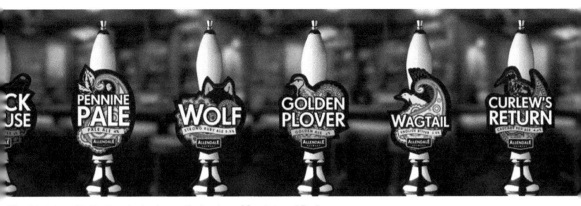

Allendale is based in Northumberland, near the borders of Cumbria and Durham, which is claimed to be 'England's last wilderness'. Their pump clips therefore evoke local wildlife from the moors – though the wolf might be wishful thinking.

Seeing how crowded the market was, Caps Off were looking for what they call 'the magpie effect … that slight glint that captures attention to make someone look closer at a brand on packed beer shelves'. 'Barry the Bear' is 'an aloof enigma that nobody knows what he is going to do next, dropping hints about the type of beer'.

New Bristol Brewery: Alfred the Gorilla was a massively popular attraction at Bristol Zoo in the 1930s, so much so that even [after] his death his taxidermic form was displayed in Bristol City Museum and Art Gallery, where he continues to act as a mascot fo[r the] city. His nifty spacesuit reflects the fact that the cans are taking him on new, exciting adventures in strange and exotic plac[es].

The guys at Manchester brewery Squawk really like birds. Different birds and different styles of illustration can help convey some of the personality of the beer; for example Corvus indicates the darkness of a stout.

FULI • DIPA

LORI • DDH IPA

IO • EKUANOT SOUR

...you're going to name your brewery after Loch Ness, there's really only one central image you can think of featuring. ...e concept is based on someone's behaviour when visiting Loch Ness for the first time: 'Did I see that, or are my eyes ...aying tricks on me?' via a simple wave pattern in which Nessie emerges.

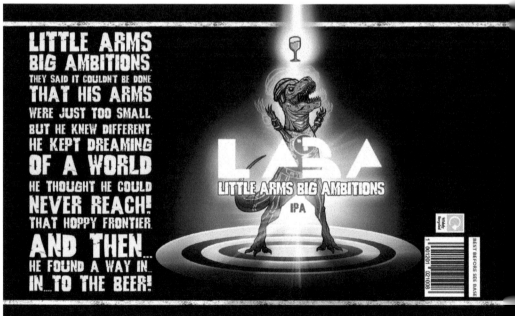

Staggeringly Good is clearly a brewery having far too much fun. If you're going to theme your brand around an animal, why not choose a Tyrannosaurus Rex and let it loose through a whole range of pop-cultural tropes?

Local history

Until the mid-twentieth century brewing was for the most part a highly localised industry. Finished beer was far more difficult to transport than the ingredients of brewing. The local terroir influenced the emergence of beer styles in ways brewers didn't understand: the hard water of Burton-on-Trent brewed wonderful, bright pale ales, whereas the soft water of Pilsen worked far better for lagers. Local beer was part of local identity: in some parts of Britain, it's still possible to get a sense of where you are by looking out for the name of the brewer that hangs on most of the roadside pub signs.

A well-executed sense of place works just as well for visitors as it does for the locals. Foreign tourists and British beer aficionados are both as likely as each other to ask for 'the local beer' when visiting a place for the first time because it is part of the experience of being there.

This has always been true of beer, but more recently, localism has become more important. Concerns over food miles and a fascination with local terroir are driving trends across the whole of food and drink. Local usually means small-scale. When researchers ask people what they believe characterises real ale and craft beer, the idea of it being locally produced is common to both. It's part of wanting to experience and reconnect with the world on a more human scale. Ideas that once seemed behind the times in a globalising economy suddenly have a fresh new relevance.

MOORHOUSES

Moorhouses was founded in Burnley in 1865, and has had its ups and downs since then. The Burnley skyline is dominated by Pendle Hill, a brooding, mystical hulk that has wrapped itself in legends over the years. In 1612 it was the location of the Pendle Witch Trials in which ten people were executed for witchcraft. Real witches, of course, cannot always be stopped by death.

Such rich local history is a wellspring of ideas for beer names. Beers like Black Cat, Blonde Witch and White Witch have long been part of the Moorhouses core range. Until recently, these beers were illustrated with sexy Halloween-costume witch imagery that was once considered fine for pump clip design, but now looks hopelessly anachronistic. A 2018 redesign swapped sexy/sexist for mystical. The outline of Pendle Hill runs through the Moorhouses logo. The witches and their familiars are eerie and unknowable. And the brewery has returned to profit and gained new listings after a long period of decline.

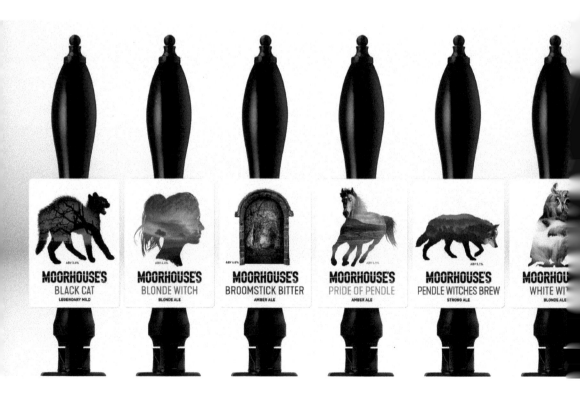

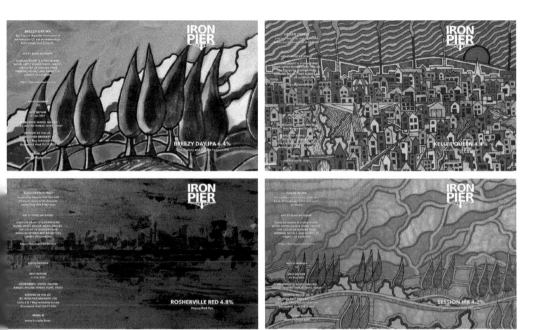

Local artist Duncan Grant is a regular in the Iron Pier taproom and specialises in images of the local area. The brewery held an exhibition of his work in the taproom before realising it would be perfect for their cans.

...ery beer in Leigh on Sea's range tells a different story about the town and its location. For example, Legra was the name of ...e town at the time of the Domesday book, while Six Little Ships pays tribute to six boats that left the town to help evacuate ...oops from Dunkirk.

BRIXTON

Local history and identity manifests itself in many different ways. The Brixton Brewery found its bold, colourful visual identity in local landmarks and architectural curiosities, elements and details of which find themselves expressed in the graphics that differentiate the beers in Brixton's core range.

The central 'B' that unites the range suggests the vibrancy and pride of Brixton, against a background of colourful abstract elements, each of which has a meaning. The sparks of Electric IPA celebrate Electric Avenue, the first street in Britain to be given electric street lighting. The rainbow-shaped bands of colour on Reliance Pale Ale reflect the Electric Lane entrance to the Reliance Arcade, a Grade II-listed market building, while the black, angular lines zig-zagging across Coldharbour lager are taken from the frontage of Southwyck House on Coldharbour Lane, a notorious example of 1970s Brutalist architecture.

Sambrooks is based in Wandsworth, and the name of its core beers have always celebrated the south London district. After a redesign, the cans now include subtle visual hints to local places and landmarks.

It's a common thing for a brewery to ask a design agency: can we maintain a strong connection with our town's heritage and tradition while also showing artwork that feels fresh and accessible to today's drinker? This is what it looks like when that tricky balancing act is a success.

Danish artist and designer Kasper Ledet works across an astonishing array of styles for To Øl,
always trying to interpret something about the character of the individual beer or range it belongs to.

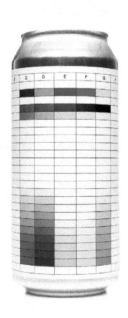

Art

The idea of the beer can as art is synonymous with craft beer in the 2020s. Visit a bottle shop and you can lose yourself in a sea of abstract impressionism.

The connection between beer and art, however, has a much longer history than the craft beer boom. The first brewer to treat their labels as artworks was actually Beck's. In 1987 the German lager brand teamed up with modern artists Gilbert and George, who created a label for a limited edition run of 2,000 bottles for an exhibition of their work at the Hayward Gallery in London. The beer sold at the exhibition was itself a part of the exhibition. Tracy Emin, Jeff Koons and Damien Hirst have also had a go, in an initiative that still happens every year. It's an extraordinary and bold project for a brand that you'd expect to be safe and conservative in its packaging.

More recently, abstract designs began as a way of drawing attention to limited edition and special release beers. Craft brewers often team up with local artists, the brand providing the frame for their work. Sometimes a single artist will become synonymous with a brewery, like the 'fifth member' of a classic band. Other brewers rotate through different artists, constantly showcasing new and interesting ideas.

The original 1987 Gilbert & Geor[ge]
Beck's bottle (above) is now a
collector's item that changes ha[nds]
for large sums. This range of des[igns]
from 2018 (left), featuring the w[ork]
of artists including Art + Believe [and]
Greg Coulton, showcases a vari[ety]
of techniques and styles from a[round]
the world of contemporary art

Mini IPA

PARTIZAN

440ml

vegan

2.7%

This mini IPA is light in strength, refreshing but with no compromise in flavour or aroma. All you would expect from our core IPA at a reduced ABV.

Ingredients: water, barley, **wheat, oats,** hops, yeast. *Allergens, including* **gluten, in bold.**

1.2 UK units
2.7% alc by vol

Art by Alec Doherty

Brewed in London, UK

partizanbrewing.co.uk

Partizan Brewing, SE16 2DB

G000.599

2nd June 2020

1 zone: best before

0 604565 338624

Lager Unfiltered

4.6%

PARTIZAN

New England Saison

4.2%

PARTIZAN

New England Pale

4.6%

PARTIZAN

Dee Dee Pale

5.5%

PARTIZAN

Double Dry Hopped Pale

rosunt Gentibus Artes means 'art empowers the people', and features on the coat of arms for Southwark. It now also atures on most Partizan labels, with the aim that Alec Doherty's original artworks do exactly that.

CLOUDWATER

How to stay the same and be different

It would be harsh but not unfair to say that when Cloudwater launched in 2015, nothing in the beer world looked like it, whereas now, almost everything does.

Following the earthquakes in craft beer design caused by BrewDog and then Beavertown, Cloudwater was the third wave of daring new design approaches that were so different that everyone else immediately copied them.

Paul Jones met Vicky Carr and Chris Shearston of Textbook Studio in Manchester's craft beer bars. Paul talked to Chris about starting a brewery that, among other things, stood apart from and rejected the macho 'bro' culture of beer, and insisted this need to be reflected in the brand's design.

Jones remarked that he wanted something closer to the elegance of a wine label than the rambunctiousness of craft beer.

Cloudwater's initial approach was to have no core range, but to introduce a new seasonal range in summer, autumn, winter and spring of each year. The idea was that each season would feature the work of a different artist on the labels. Change was rapid, and soon Cloudwater had produced scores of different beers, each with its own design. Eventually, the pace slowed down, and the visual approach now changes yearly.

The beauty and intrigue of Cloudwater's design approach has been widely celebrated. 'It's just all about textures,' says Chris Shearsto He's fascinated by visual depictions of texture.

But even more than that, he believes it's the boring bits that actually make it work. 'The way the information is displayed is absolutely crucial,' he tells me. 'Certain elements always have to stay the same: the logo is always the same size and always in the same space. The font for the name of the beer never changes, and it's a simple one so it can be consistent across the website and all other communication.'

Paul Jones still collaborates very closely on the design, and often takes photographs himself which end up being detailed in the artwork. 'He carries a camera around with him all the time and just snaps anything he thinks is interesting,' says Chris. 'I'm so strict about the layout that now, when he looks through the viewfinder, he has a sense of where the logo will be and frames the shot accordingly.'

In 2019, and now amid a sea of cans displaying the work of local artists held within a branded frame, Cloudwater zagged again and introduced a permanent core range for the first time. 'There's more information on the front of the cans,' says Chris. 'The idea is that you should be able to read it clearly in a fridge behind the bar.'

So here is Cloudwater re-embracing the core principles of conventional commercial packaging design, although it's highly debatable that they ever deviated from those principles in the first place. The design has always tried to stand out and be distinctive, but it's always been very clearly branded, consistent, and yet always changing.

Canopy commission different artists and then shake things up, splitting all their figures into three to form 'creatures' that combine their work. You can even create your own on the website.

Artist John Robinson collaborates as closely as possible with Boundary brewer Matthew Dick, to the extent that he has a st___ in the brewery. 'Matthew makes his beer with certain characteristics and qualities to which I respond in the paintings. Som__ it's the other way around. The Boundary paintings are a unique project and there is a flow of ideas back and forth,' he says.

Whiplash: Artist Sophie de Vere uses a mix of photography and collage on the white canvasses supplied to her by her partner's brewery.

Wylam's one-off beers are carefully considered in their naming and are usually a comment on the state of the world. The brewery works closely with artist Sally Linsdell, providing a narrative and direction behind each beer, then batting ideas back and forth until 'it sings as we both see it'.

The inspiration behind both beer and design is that whoever we are and whatever our ambitions, nothing feels as comforting as when we get together to share a pint, a meal, a conversation. It comes from the expression 'If you go straight long enough you end up where you were'.

Illustration

Illustration might be a broad category that incorporates and overlaps with some others such as cartoons and popular culture, but we're singling it out here specifically to talk about illustration as a particular approach to visuals, as opposed to patterns, photography, textures and more abstract forms of art.

This is about drawing rather than painting, and it's about how drawing in a particular style – giving visual elements a cohesive look, feel, mood or aesthetic – can say as much, if not more, about the brand than the actual subject being depicted.

It's striking looking at some of the brands in this section how you can instantly identify a Mikkeller, Anspach & Hobday or Tiny Rebel beer just from the signature style of the artist. There are as many different styles of drawing as there are people who can draw, so illustration is a great way of making your brand look unlike anyone else's.

Even if it's created on computer rather than drawn by hand, a distinctive illustrative style still suggests a very human element of individuality. It allows for story-telling and nuance, and can create a particular emotion or association with a historical period, place, or a different aspect of popular culture. But on top of that, when people like an illustrative style, they really warm to it – it's more likely to inspire genuine affection than cooler, more abstract approaches.

Artist Keith Shore was hired in 2010 to design one label for Mikkeller. He had little interest in beer at the time, so his design looked unlike anything else on the shelf. He's designed just about every Mikkeller label since.

The sirens of Greek mythology inspired the Siren as a concept. Just as their voices were said to entwine into a complex, layered melody, so do the ingredients that go into making great beer.

Kev Grey creates bold black-and-white illustrations that draw on classic tattoo themes and old-school skate art, with a healthy sprinkling of humour. His designs differ wildly from can to can, but they all scream Black Iris.

Artist Simon Gane took advantage of Burning Sky's move to 440ml cans to grow the canvas for his cast of characters that feel like they've stepped out of French comics, creating a world that's different from the competition and yet naggingly familiar.

Bermondsey brewer Anspach & Hobday base their business around the concept of 'traditional styles in a new way'. Each design illustrates this with a pair of characters – one Victorian, one modern – with the illustration style evoking an age when London was the brewing capital of the world.

The idea at the heart of Wiper & True's designs is that fermentation is a natural process that has (to an extent) been harnessed by humanity to create something extraordinary. Each illustration depicts another expression of humans conquering or interacting with nature.

Founders Brad and Gazz had a clear idea of a brand they wanted to be 'a bit rough around the edges, urban and grungy, rebellious but still soft deep down'. They saw the artwork of artist Taz on an episode of the Marvel TV series *Jessica Jones*, and persuaded her to come and work for them to bring their ideas to life in the form of a distressed-looking bear.

Ampersand keep their core range to a strict black-on-white colour scheme. First comes the name of the beer, then comes a minimalist, cute illustration that brings that name to life.

Into The Haze, our IPA. Soft, juicy, citrus and tropical-fruit laden IPA in our house style. This beer has a clean malt structure, peachy yeast esters, and the saturated presence of Citra and Simcoe. Refreshing, clean and beautiful to drink!

Please keep this can refrigerated to preserve the flavour profile intended.

Hops fade quickly - drink now!

This beer is Vegan friendly.

UNFILTERED
UNPASTEURISED
UNFINED

Best before: see base

Brewed and canned at
DEYA Brewing Company,
Unit 27,
Lansdown Industrial Estate,
Gloucester Road,
Cheltenham, GL51 8PL.
Tel: 01242269189
Twitter/Insta: @deyabrewery
www.deyabrewing.com

www.drinkaware.co.uk

IPA   ABV 6.2%

3.1 UK UNITS

5 060771 950022   500 ML

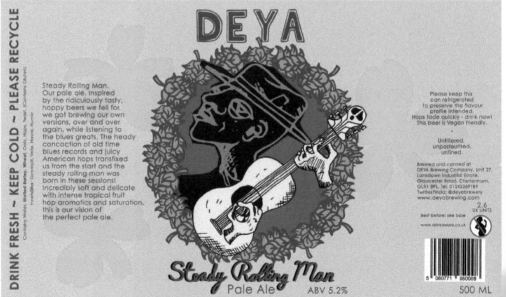

Steady Rolling Man. Our pale ale. Inspired by the ridiculously tasty, hoppy beers we fell for, we got brewing our own versions, over and over again, while listening to the blues greats. The heady concoction of old time blues records and juicy American hops transfixed us from the start and the steady rolling man was born in these sessions! Incredibly soft and delicate with intense tropical fruit hop aromatics and saturation, this is our vision of the perfect pale ale.

Please keep this can refrigerated to preserve the flavour profile intended. Hops fade quickly - drink now! This beer is Vegan friendly.

Unfiltered, unpasteurised, unfined.

Brewed and canned at DEYA Brewing Company, Unit 27, Lansdown Industrial Estate, Gloucester Road, Cheltenham, GL51 8PL. Tel: 01242269189 Twitter/Insta: @deyabrewery www.deyabrewing.com

Best before: see base

www.drinkaware.co.uk

2.6 UK UNITS

Steady Rolling Man
Pale Ale   ABV 5.2%

5 060771 950008   500 ML

All Deya's designs are created by in-house artist Thom Hobson. The aesthetic aims for illustrative and quirky while being clean, easy to read and modern, reflecting a brand that's fresh and clean, but also playful and fun.

Graphics and geometric patterns

The human brain is trained to spot patterns. Patterns are symbols that repeat to cover a surface, and when we spot patterns, we feel calm. We recognise order, and that order makes looking at patterns a pleasant experience. It's why we have patterns in tiles, mosaics and wallpaper: they create structure that makes us feel safe.

The most popular patterns in craft beer design at the time of writing are geometric patterns, where simple shapes repeat in grid formation to create a strict sense of order. Becoming more solid, a pattern might merge to form a sense of texture rather than separate objects, or the pattern might be scattered to create a looser, less formal arrangement.

Patterns and graphics are often a blank slate onto which the viewer can impose a meaning, or not worry about meaning at all. They can convey meaning in ways we don't even register consciously, and can symbolise moods, emotions, movement and ideas. Some are futuristic, while others playfully evoke 1970s kitchens or your granny's wallpaper.

The danger is that they are easy to do, and when so many people use them they can all merge into one. Here are some that manage to own various abstract patterns in graphics in ways that feel distinctive.

When Fourpure provided a house pale ale for Tate Modern, graphic artist Peter Saville was asked to design the can. As with Saville's graphic identity for the gallery, the design represents the shape of the Tate Modern building.

In a marriage of traditional inspiration and contemporary art, logo marque and design abstractions that spring from it are based on a representation of a wool-weighing scale used in framework knitting, which Framework found in the Wigston Framework Knitting Museum. It has been their muse since day one.

LOST IN CONTROL
DIPA (IDAHO 7 CRYO CITRA SABRO GALAXY) - 8.2% ABV

PINBALL (B/W TRACK BREWING CO)
NEIPA (GALAXY CITRA AMARILLO) 6.7% ABV

POCKET ROCKET
TINY IPA (CITRA SIMCOE IDAHO 7) - 2.7% ABV

PULL TOGETHER
TINY PALE (CASCADE CITRA CRYO SIMCOE) - 2.8% ABV

SCREWBALL
LEMON AND LIME BERLINER WEISSE - 3.5% ABV

SHOUT MODE
KVEIK DIPA (CITRA SIMCOE CRYO MOSAIC) - 8.0% ABV

owling Hops is proudly a product of its environment. Hackney, and Hackney Wick in particular, provides plenty of artistic spiration, from the sheer amount of street art and murals to the boss's love of soul music. Sometimes the beer names me first and influence the artwork, sometimes the other way around.

Beerblefish works with a social enterprise that aims to help ex-military personnel into civilian employment, and this led to a design inspired by the graphics used in 'dazzle ships' in the First World War. When the three main beers are stood in the right order, the label frontages make up the whole fish of the name.

Inspired by the founder's love of techno, Overtone's design is inspired by the cutting-edge graphics and cult status of iconic record labels. The patterns are inspired by the brewery name: overtones are frequencies that alter the qualities of a sound, so designers Thirst use lines and colour to create illusions that change the qualities of the label before your eyes.

As the name suggests, Atom are scientists by trade and want to celebrate science through their beer. Their visual design is based in information representation in science, and represents characteristics of the beers as data visualisation. In their words, 'Data representation can be called the art of science.'

As a craft brewer for whom cask is the dominant format, Bristol's Tapestry Brewery's pump clips have to work hard. The text layout is clean, simple and informative, while patterns are used sparingly, catching the eye without overpowering the information. A subtle line texture adds a further fabric-like depth to the design.

NORTH

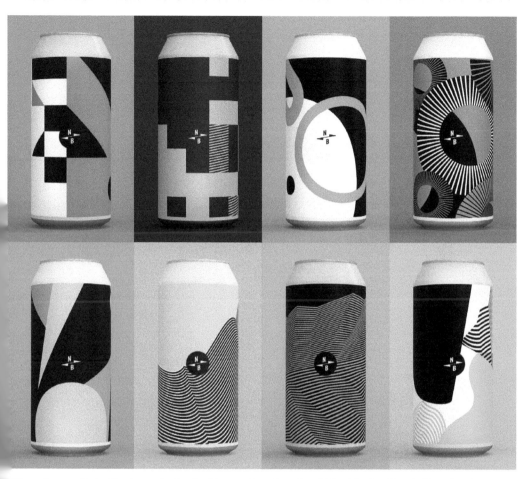

When James Ockelford was tasked with creating the visual identity for North Brewing Co, he wanted it to reflect the eclecticism that he had loved in North Bar, the pioneering Leeds craft beer bar that had given birth to the brewery. 'I'd hear music by Aphex Twin or Can, drink Belgian and Dutch beer and talk to complete strangers about music and live projections at gigs,' he says.

At the time of North's launch in 2015, the prevailing aesthetics in craft beer were punk and heavy metal. James wanted to go somewhere different. 'I had a wide variety of influences,' he says, and proceeds to list some of them: mid-century modernism, Dada, African textile design, early Soviet space race stuff, artists such as Brigette Riley, Franco Grignani, Ellsworth Kelly and Gary Hume, folk tales, Joy Division, Stanley Kubrick, retrofuturism and Saul Bass.

'A lot of my design influences are fifty-plus years old,' says James. 'Without dissecting the psychology of this too much… basically there's an optimism about looking to the past – back to a time when the future was imagined with some optimism.'

Aberdeen's six°north make strong use of colour and experimental techniques to communicate the style and taste for their largely Belgian-inspired beers: dark colour schemes are used for dark beers, bright and vibrant for more hop-forward style

Pop culture and kitsch

In an earlier chapter about how branding works, we talked about the study of semiotics: analysing signs as signifier and signified.

In traditional beer, the semiotic system is pretty straightforward: silver, gold, gothic fonts, medals, crowns and shields all signify authority and tradition. Pastoral scenes, hops, barley, shire horses and brewing equipment in turn signify that beer is a natural, crafted product. As a system of signs, it's quite inward looking: it's signifying beer.

Modern craft beer takes a different view. It works on the assumption that you already know you're buying a beer, and is confident that the packaging doesn't need to remind you of the fact. So instead, it looks outwards. It uses a system of signs that emphasises beer as a social and cultural product, which of course it is.

That's why many craft beer brands gleefully play with visuals that connect beer to rock, heavy metal or punk music, to film, science fiction, fantasy, fashion, prison or navy tattoos, comics and any other trashy manifestation of pop culture they can think of. Did I say trashy? There's not really any such thing any more. The boundaries between high and low culture have been erased. Art is judged on its own terms.

Beer exists in a broader cultural context. Very few drinkers sit and analyse the content and flavour profile of their beer while drinking it with friends in the pub. You talk about music, what was on TV last night, or which is the best Star Wars film. While some craft beers may not look anything like beer any more, they're just trying to join in, or maybe even inspire, the conversation.

SIGNATURE BREW

Signature Brew began in 2011 with a bunch of music fans who were so frustrated at the terrible beer available at live gig venues, they resolved to do something about it. They began with the idea of collaborating with bands to create beers those artists wanted to drink, and have since worked with over twenty-five acts, including Alt-J, Mogwai, Frank Turner and Idles. Each of these beers had a limited shelf life, so in 2016 – a year after opening their own brewery after previously brewing with friends – they launched their core 'Signature' range. Instead of being linked to any one band or style of music, these had to be relevant to any music fan, so the design, like the naming scheme, is inspired by the everyday business of working in live music. These cans are based on the passes that crew wear in and around the venue.

Launched in 2013, everything about Weird Beard stems from the shared passions of its founders: heavy metal and horror films. Each beer has a character designed for it called a 'Lupin'. Everyone working at the brewery eventually ends up as a lupin.

Sometimes design can be as simple as commissioning your favourite illustrator. One of Maule's founders had worked with Kate Prior, who's created an upbeat, colourful range of wild characters and positive names – Lucky, Wonder, Fantastic and Smashing.

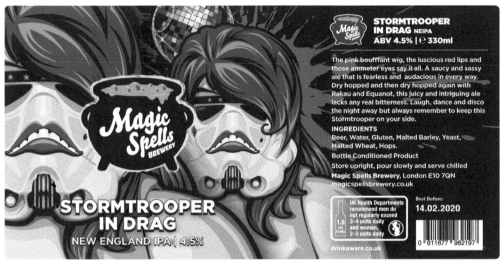

STORMTROOPER IN DRAG NEIPA
ABV 4.5% | ℮ 330ml

The pink boufffant wig, the luscious red lips and those ammeter eyes say it all. A saucy and sassy ale that is fearless and audacious in every way. Dry hopped and then dry hopped again with Rakau and Equanot, this juicy and intriguing ale lacks any real bitterness. Laugh, dance and disco the night away but always remember to keep this Stormtrooper on your side.

INGREDIENTS
Beer, Water, Gluten, Malted Barley, Yeast, Malted Wheat, Hops.

Bottle Conditioned Product
Store upright, pour slowly and serve chilled
Magic Spells Brewery, London E10 7QN
magicspellsbrewery.co.uk

UK Health Departments recommend men do not regularly exceed 3–4 units daily and women, 2–3 units daily
1.5 UK Units

drinkaware.co.uk

Best Before:
14.02.2020

0 611677 962197

STORMTROOPER IN DRAG
NEW ENGLAND IPA | 4.5%

BIZARRE LOVE TRIANGLE IPA
ABV 5% | ℮ 500ml

Every time you drink a few, you feel shot right through with a bolt of blue. A Bizarre Love Triangle of Azacca, Columbus and Simcoe hops, this passionate India Pale Ale is distinctive, charismatic and full of flavour.

INGREDIENTS
Beer, Water, Gluten, Malted Barley, Yeast, Malted Wheat, Hops.

Bottle Conditioned Product
Store upright, pour slowly and serve chilled
Magic Spells Brewery, London E10 7QN
magicspellsbrewery.co.uk / @magicspellsbrew

UK Health Departments recommend men do not regularly exceed 3–4 units daily and women, 2–3 units daily
2.5 UK Units

drinkaware.co.uk

Best Before:
15.08.2020

0 611677 962227

BIZARRE LOVE TRIANGLE
IPA | 5%

Magic Spells come up with a beer and a name for it before briefing graphic designer James Mayall. He's then free to boldly go wherever the name takes him.

Designer Luke McLean has lived in Hackney for twenty years. He describes his aesthetic for London Fields as 'some kind of alternative 6am acid-tinged world. Maybe London Fields itself.'

Double-Barrelled use a simple, clean template which they can then overlay on a rich array of images to combine sophisticated consistency with an eclectic visual feel.

Williams Bros 'totem' theme began as a project to develop a new range of 500ml cans, a format known informally in the beer trade as 'tall boys'. These developed into an abstract family, each of whom will have their own distinctive character, underpinned by a common DNA.

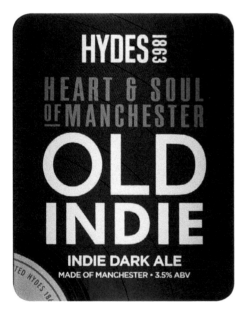

Hydes is a long-established brewery in the heart of Manchester. By drawing on the city's unparalleled music culture, it makes its cask ale instantly look relevant. For an independent brewery, this was an open goal.

Minimalism

It's an obvious, yet very effective, strategy in any kind of marketing to watch where everyone else is going, and then head off in a different direction. When the shelves are exploding in a riot of shape, colour, texture and noise, less is more, and quiet is the new loud.

Minimalism began as an artistic movement after the Second World War, and was championed most prominently in architecture and music. It involves the removal of extra design elements, paring down until what is left is the core of the creation at hand, until there's nothing left that can be removed.

Minimalism in branding twists this slightly. Strictly speaking, it doesn't take every unnecessary element away, but it does follow a clean aesthetic that focuses your attention on the absolute essentials. It's as much about what isn't there as what is, making bold use of empty space to allow design elements to breathe and stand out, in a way that can actually make the absence of something feel like a feature in its own right.

Like art, minimalism has a longer history in beer design than you might think, but is currently enjoying a great revival. It suggests a quiet confidence, and a sense of premiumness; a beer that doesn't have to try too hard to get your attention.

The Japanese are renowned experts of minimalism, and introduced the trend to beer packaging decades before the modern craft beer scene adopted it.

THE KERNEL

Quiet is the new loud

The Kernel's iconic labelling reminds me in some ways of Bill Hicks's routine about advertising and marketing. Bill rages that people who work in these professions should kill themselves, and then imagines a marketing executive in the audience saying, 'Hey, Bill's going for the anti-marketing dollar. Good move, that's a big market just now.'

Evin O'Riordain honestly wasn't trying to be this clever when he decided to use plain brown paper and stencilled lettering as his packaging approach. He just wanted the packaging to say what the beer is, as he puts it, 'to keep quiet so the beer speaks louder.'

This is typical of a brewer who is revered in the UK craft beer scene for his excellent beers, and just as loved for his distinctly low-key approach. Evin is quiet and thoughtful and considers his words carefully. While he's happy to chat about beer with anyone, he doesn't seek the limelight for himself – he's the opposite of the idea of a 'rock star brewer'. In that sense, the packaging is an extension of his own personality – which is exactly what great packaging design should do.

'My wife has a background in design so she knew what she was doing with it,' he explains.

'When we first started off, we really were using hand stencils on brown parcel paper. When we scaled up the brewery and got a bottling line we no longer had to do our labels by hand, but we decided to keep the design.'

Eight years on, Kernel's visual identity – if you can even call it that – is still hailed as a design classic. It's distinctive in an overcrowded, shouty market. It's never had to change, and it's impossible to imagine it changing. Its quiet strength is highlighted by the fact that since it launched, some rivals have overhauled their visual identity three or four times in a struggle to remain contemporary, relevant and visible.

This is true minimalism: there's nothing on the label that isn't essential. You can't take anything else away from it without stopping it from working properly. And that means no design agency can improve on it – or copy it. 'We've been told by friends overseas that in some countries there are brewers who've basically copied us,' says Evin, 'but no one in the UK has done anything quite like it.'

If there's an edition of this book published in another eight years' time, I fully expect the Kernel will still be in it, unchanged, and just as admired as it is now.

MARBLE

Marble is one of those curious breweries that began life as a traditional cask ale brewery over twenty years ago, and has somehow balanced that effortlessly with being a contemporary craft brewer creating innovative beers while not losing its appeal as a brewer of excellent real ales.

Its packaging reflects this: while some seasonals and specials play in bright, colourful, contemporary craft territory, the core range manages to be minimalist in a particularly friendly way. Names are often descriptive, fonts are open and warm, and colours are bright and inviting. The whole combines to create a particularly strong brand identity from very few elements, which remains contemporary without alienating anyone.

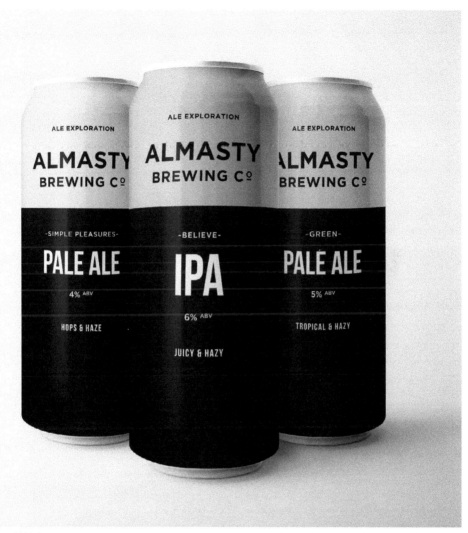

Going into the 2020 Coronavirus lockdown, Almasty was a cask ale brewery with no packaged beer, and a brand-new canning line in shipping crates. In designing cans to launch under these circumstances, they aimed to stand out with simple art and design and clear information on the beer contained within.

Coast specialises exclusively in 0% ABV craft beers. They realised eyes were used across design, but not in beer.
The wide-open eye represents being fully awake, present and sober. The eye also suggests a modernist gaze on the future.

The simple graphics on Drygate's labels represent the character of the beer: the fruity blast of a sour or the hoppy impact
of a double IPA.

Nostalgia

Big Beer is made in soulless factories. We like to imagine that, back in the old days, when things were done on a smaller, more human scale, the beer was better, just like the world itself was better.

Like so much nostalgia, this probably isn't true: beers now are certainly cleaner and more consistent than they were 150 years ago, and even if they're wild and funky, they're wild and funky in a way the brewer wants them to be.

But old-time imagery comforts us: the past is fixed and known while the present is uncertain and the future is scary. New beers can put down roots based on authenticity or provenance, using nostalgia to remind you that they've always been here, or make you think they've been around for a lot longer than they have.

Craft beer is nostalgic in a different way from a lot of other branches of the craft movement. Whereas the wooden spinning wheel beloved of craft shops is a symbol of a pre-industrial neverland, craft evokes nostalgia for the industrial age itself, with breweries in railway arches and beer bars sporting bare brick walls, exposed heating ducts and filament light bulbs.

Whatever period a beer chooses to evoke, nostalgia-themed visuals suggest a time when things were done properly. Done well, it's a quick way to build trust in a brand.

ANCHOR

Anchor is famously known as the genesis of the US craft beer revolution. It was almost defunct when Fritz Maytag bought a stake in it in 1965, and it took him years to make it a viable business. Anchor's flagship was steam beer, an old style unique to California. As Maytag got himself established, he revived porter and introduced English-style ales.

All these styles looked to the past at a time when the US was undergoing the great Beer Wars, as big lager brands battled it out for supremacy. Maytag very consciously chose to have his labels hand drawn, with the lettering echoing John Baskerville's eighteenth-century typefaces.

At the time, the logic was that craft beers were handmade, therefore the label should reflect that. The aesthetics of modern craft beer design may have moved on, but Anchor remains a classic that hasn't wavered in its design approach in over forty years.

...udvar is owned by the Czech government and in 2020 did a brand refresh to proclaim its status as the flagship of 'the ...public of Beer'. The new identity takes its stylistic cues from the brewery's archive, dating back to its founding in 1895.

'You know the brand is resonating with your audience when label artwork starts showing up as tattoos in your Instagram feed,' says design agency Ebbing Branding on their website. Odells created an instant sense of heritage with its old-fashioned yet humorous label designs.

Nostalgia can be linked to popular culture as well as brewing heritage. Here, Cornwall's Firebrand (founded 2008) use colour and graphics to strongly evoke the 1960s.

Shepherd Neame stakes a claim to be Britain's oldest brewery. Their 'classics collection' was created by decoding recipes from old brewing books, and label designs were based heavily on what they looked like a century ago, creating a sense of reassurance and trust.

Moor's nostalgia is subtle: a long-established English brewery rescued by an American craft brewer, the look it went for was timeless rather than old-fashioned. In 2020 the look was refreshed and gently simplified, making it more recognisable.

JW Lees is a 200-year-old brewery having to compete with a wave of younger, hipper craft breweries. Working closely with Manchester lettering artist Darren Newman, design agency Squad evoked a long and colourful history in a style that has urgent contemporary appeal.

Brand worlds

Sometimes, a design scheme is so big it stretches
beyond the label or can on which it sits. Individual
elements recur or even join up to suggest something
greater. They give us the impression of a fully
realised brand world, a place that exists – at least in
someone's imagination – and which is populated by
people or magical creatures, where things happen
on a day-to-day basis. The images we see are not just
stand-alone designs; they are snapshots of different
characters or events, scenes from an ongoing story.

The great thing about a brand world is that it
invites us to fill in the gaps, to imagine the rest of
the adventure from the scene we've witnessed.
The distinctive aesthetic that defines a brand world
can spread and grow from packaging onto websites,
T-shirts, beer mats, delivery vans and poster sites.
When done well, you can see an image from that
world, shorn of any branding or other context, and
immediately know where it comes from. This is
visual design (often illustrated), type, logo, all
coming together to create something that lives
and breathes on its own.

BEAVERTOWN

Resistance is futile

The story of how Nick Dwyer accidentally ended up as the author of the most iconic beer brand identity of the last decade is well-known. Dwyer had trained as an illustrator and was working at the brewpub that was Beavertown's first base, when founder Logan Plant spotted some of the doodles Dwyer was idly sketching. Plant immediately knew that this was what he wanted on what were then bottles, and later, cans. The rest is dayglo history.

'Well, to be honest, I gamed that a little,' confesses Dwyer, now Beavertown's long-standing creative director. 'I just might have had some fully done sketchbooks waiting for the right moment to grab Logan's attention.'

Beavertown's look and feel was at least as responsible as the (very fine) beer in making it one of the most desirable craft beer brands of the mid-2010s, and for the depths of anguish created among a section of its fans when Beavertown sold a minority stake to Heineken in 2018. The son of a rock star and his lead designer had created a brand that was as cool as any music legend. The pain of being called a sell-out was no doubt eased by 500% growth in sales over the ensuing twelve months.

As a student, Dwyer specialised in illustration rather than just graphic design, and his obsession with fifties-style spacemen long predates his association with Beavertown. 'Illustrators back then were always looking to

hock people in a brutal, animalist way,' he says. 'ou wanted it to have an energy. You wanted s many people to see it as possible.'

When the visual style that Dwyer escribes as 'Dan Dare and Thunderbirds for dults' is many things at once. It's sci-fi, and 's also comic. It's futuristic in a very retro ay. It's challenging and controversial, but omehow also friendly – you can't help but

have a sneaky affection for a ray-gun-toting skeleton in a space suit. It didn't just look like no other beer brand; it didn't look like commercial branding at all.

'We didn't really go against the rulebook,' Dwyer recalls, 'It was more a question of not knowing there *was* a rulebook. It's as if we turned up to a party we weren't invited to, and we just happened to be dressed exactly right.'

(cont.)

Dwyer's style is so unique that you can spot what professional design agencies would call one of Beavertown's 'visual assets' entirely out of context. If you saw a spaceman or a skeleton on a wall, T-shirt or the side of a van, you'd know it was Beavertown even without words or a logo. It's this that makes me think of Beavertown's design aesthetic as a brand world: a crazy, action-packed place that we're seeing random snippets from.

Incredibly, at the time of writing the branding is eight years old. Some other breweries who began by aping Beavertown's approach have rebranded two or three times since then. Beavertown still feels like a benchmark of craft beer design. And as the brand now reaches a broader mainstream audience, the monsters are assaulting the senses of a brand-new market for the first time.

Hackney Brewery's designer
Pete Fowler is famous for his
work with bands such as Super
Furry Animals, and Hackney
Brewery speak of him as one of
the team, closely linked with the
overall direction of the brewer.
Fowler creates seemingly
straightforward designs based on
individual beers, but there's more
to them than meets the eye. He
weaves a lot of subtle cues into
each design, from the founders'
mild obsession with Batman
through to small nods to the
brewery's unique identity: the
year it was founded, the brewery
dogs and where everyone first
met, as well as providing hints
that link to the next beer.
Everything is made cohesive by a
strong colour palette and design
rules that nearly always feature
clouds, mountains and lightning.

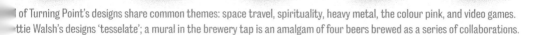

ll of Turning Point's designs share common themes: space travel, spirituality, heavy metal, the colour pink, and video games.
ttie Walsh's designs 'tesselate'; a mural in the brewery tap is an amalgam of four beers brewed as a series of collaborations.

LOST & GROUNDED

Telling stories

Before they finally laid down their roots in Bristol and opened Lost & Grounded in July 2016, Alex Troncoso and Annie Clements had lived in twenty-one houses in twenty years. They felt lost. And then, finally, they found somewhere that felt like home.

The couple has a few years on most people who start up new craft breweries. They've seen and experienced the world and have stories to relate. Now they're telling those stories through the beer itself, and through the haunting imagery they use to sell them.

'We quite deliberately talk about being *brewers* rather than a *brewery*,' says Annie. 'It's all about the people – if it's not, it's just a shed. We had the chance to build something in our own image so we were quite careful about what we wanted that to be.'

The pair settled on four words that they wanted to be the basis of everything the business did: humble, inclusive, clever and raw. They talked about this to local illustrator Alexia Tucker and designer Sam Davis and asked for a design that was quiet and intimate. 'A lot of other breweries were shouting in their design. We wanted something softer, more intriguing,' says Annie.

Tucker's illustration style is a story in itself: Alex and Annie lived in Belgium for a while, and the art on their labels gives a nod to Belgian-style graphic novels.

All the labels for the core range link up to create a broad panorama, in which recurring characters appear. The main one is the winged hippo from the main brewery logo, carrying the weight of the world on his shoulders. 'The hippo is humble and determined,' says Annie, 'A hippo might not be a rock star, but if you get in its way it will fuck you up!'

On the brewery's flagship Keller Pils, the hippo is rowing across Lake Constance, near Tettnang in Germany, and the green lines on the hill in the background are, according to Alex, the Tettnanger hops used in the beer. On Hop Hand Fallacy he's being tempted into losing money on cards. Initially he's nowhere to be seen on Apophenia, L&G's astounding Belgian Tripel, but look closely at the island in the centre of the label and you realise it's the hippo on his side, fast asleep after one too many of this 8.8% ABV beer.

The racoon on No Rest For Dancers represents Annie herself, and tells a particular story of feeling lonely while the couple were living in Belgium, and getting out the beers,

turning up the music and dancing the anxiety away at 5pm on a Friday. Meanwhile, Running With Sceptres represents the idea that a sceptre may be associated with royalty, but we all carry our own version of one – each of us is as unique and special as the animals marching up the hill.

Now I'm getting into it, I suggest a few details and interpretations of my own: aren't those houses on the hill in the background of Hop Hand Fallacy the brightly painted houses of Clifton Wood in Bristol?

Alex and Annie smile and don't give a direct answer. 'It's like the lyrics of a song,' they say. 'You can appreciate the art without having to know all the detail. The important thing is that we ourselves know the full story.'

Every time a beer becomes a permanent part of the range, it gets a design that makes it part of the panorama. The story continues. Will it have a happy ending?

'Let's hope that the hippo gets a holiday one of these days,' says Alex, and suddenly, I realise which animal I'm talking to.

Inspired by the outdoors and their love of adventure, Wander Beyond developed a surreal and exciting world to reflect the flavour of their beers. Hops climb mountains, barrels dwell in caves and mischievous fruits roam free.

'it does what it says on the tin'

Beneath the Label

Fonts

The design of fonts to go on the bar has progressed in a way not dissimilar to an arms race. Not too long ago, the wooden hand pumps from which real ale is served were the tallest things on the bar. As discussed earlier, keg beers began as small, plastic illuminated boxes on the bar. But as the number of brands on the bar exploded, fonts grew bigger and more ornate. Now, a premium lager font is likely to tower over the real ale handpulls. Cleverly, this means the illuminated logo of the beer will be at eye level for many drinkers, illuminated and shining in your eyes to grab your attention. Some fonts have chilled glycol running through them so they they 'sweat' or even gather a coating of ice, upping the yearning for that first ice-cold hit of refreshment.

The downside is that pints have to be passed carefully through a forest of gleaming chrome and steel, often catching and spilling and having to be topped up. Sometimes customer and server struggle to make eye contact, and the whole process of buying a beer can become over-complicated. We've reached the point where fonts really can't grow any bigger, which is why many bars have instituted a scorched earth policy of scrapping individual fonts and instead installing generic T-bars and 'goalpost' fonts carrying multiple taps, each of which only has room for an illuminated lens showing the logo of the beer being served.

This has all left cask ale at a disadvantage. Cask is still served most commonly from a traditional handpull, which draws beer up from the cellar by manual pulling. Because they need to be pulled back while serving a beer, it's not really practical to make them much bigger than they already are. They need to maintain a shape and texture that doesn't make pulling any more difficult, so cask ale is limited in how far it can innovate in design terms. This has been costly for cask: studies that track the eye movement of customers approaching the bar show that cask is spotted last, if at all.

Some brands have introduced bespoke fonts in their own pub estates where their beers are on permanently. These might be finished in chrome, brass or ceramic, and can be smooth tubes rather than traditional curved wooden handpulls. But this isn't practical for most pubs, who are constantly rotating their cask beer lines. When they do so, they change the badge or pump clip that fits around the base of the tap handle and is held in place with a screwed bracket.

So all that most cask ale brands can do to attempt a greater degree of standout is make their pump clips ever more ornate. While a rotating guest ale traditionally has a carboard oval, core range pump clips are growing ever larger and taking on a variety of shapes such as shields and scrolls. They're also acquiring an extra dimension, with embossing making them quite chunky. It's another battle in the attention-grabbing arms race, which unintentionally makes the worst culprits look bloated, and like they're taking themselves far too seriously. Designs can often look far better when they have been simplified and taken back to basics.

Peroni has taken the of trend of large, eye-catching fonts possibly as far as it can go in the typical pub. The bespoke Peroni font is 651mm high, and is designed to look like a sail. It makes particularly clever use of the depth of the bar. Straight on, it's slender and elegant, but from the side, it's much more eye-catching.

In the US, draught beer branding takes the form of bespoke tap handles that screw into the base, and can be changed when beers change, rather than pump clips affixed to the front of the font. London Fields has adopted that approach in the UK for its own taproom, with each handle being a figure from the beer's range of personalities featured on the labels.

Chiltern's solution to standout on the bar is so simple it works far better than it probably should: each pump clip depicts the pint the pump is serving, in the shape of a pint glass. It's curiously compelling.

YOUNG'S

Young's had various problems with its visual identity: like many long-established cask ale brands, craft beer was making it look old fashioned and lacking in relevance. The range was lacking consistency: when the same beers appeared in cask and in bottle, they had quite different designs. Finally, the cask ale pump clips, cut distinctively in the shape of the brewery's ram mascot, were creating some disconnect with the idea of Young's being a leading London brewer.

Design agency Kingdom & Sparrow introduced a coherent design across all formats. It made London a part of the identity with a new typeface inspired by Edward Johnston's letterforms for the London Underground (1916), with added serifs. The ram is now more active and challenging, leaping over the modern London skyline. The colours are bolder and more contemporary.

This all combines to have the effect of greater standout and a more modern feel, without seeming to try too hard or be something it's not – well, aside from the fact that Young's is no longer actually brewed in London.

Bottles

The container that beer is packaged in or served from can be far more than just the receptacle on which the label is fixed. Every single part of the package can be used to say something about the brand it contains. Many of these tweaks and details come at an extra cost, so they often signify premiumness, a sense that this is a beer worth spending more on: at least as far as the brewer is concerned.

There are strict conventions in beer bottling. As previously discussed, premium bottled ales are packaged in 500ml brown bottles, while lagers are packaged in 330ml green bottles.

The colour of the glass is all about restricting UV light penetration, which can create a degradation of the hops known as 'light strike' or 'skunking'. Brown is most effective at this but is considered dull and old-fashioned. Green is not as good, but has some effect. However, research shows that drinkers overwhelmingly prefer clear glass, which makes the beer look more appetising and refreshing, but almost certainly means the beer inside will be light-struck. Clear glass bottles are a signal that a brewer has prioritised the presentation of the beer over preserving its quality. Fortunately for them, it's a lot harder to taste this degradation in the beer if you drink it ice-cold and straight from the bottle so you're not getting any aroma. Stick a wedge of lime in the top, and it becomes very difficult to taste just how ruined the beer is.

The size and shape of a bottle can be highly effective in positioning a brand. Any beer drinker who holidayed in France as a teenager will have fond memories of 250ml 'stubbies', the perfect size for a quick refreshing hit. Its relative, the

'steinie', similarly squat but fatter, is synonymous with Belgian beers. The 750ml bottle, known in the US craft beer circles as a 'bomber', borrows wine cues to suggest a stronger beer that's perfect for sharing, particularly over a meal.

There's a general trend towards light-weighting bottles for environmental reasons. The problem is that this makes a brand feel cheaper, but it can be countered by bespoke embossing of bottles. Embossing usually consists of the brand name or logo, and is beloved of designers who talk about how the consumer can touch the brand as well as seeing it.

Other tricks include putting a ceramic or plastic coating over the glass, or printing straight onto the bottle rather than affixing a label, all of which are seen as premium cues. Other finishes on labels include metallic paint or paper, or spot varnish, to again accentuate texture.

Finally, the closure on a bottle provides opportunities for smart finishing touches. Crown caps are easy and effective, and therefore universal. They can be a surface to provide an extra bit of branding, and some designers even add hidden messages on the inside. Cork and wire cages suggest a beer that should be considered on a par with wine or champagne, while either a crown cap or a cork can be covered with foil, wax, or a paper seal to signify some kind of special reserve.

You can immediately recognise certain Belgian beer styles from the shape of their bottle: So strong are these associatio that if breweries from anywhe else want to brew beers in the styles then buying the right-sh bottle does an awful lot of wo in communicating information about the beer.

(right) Crown caps are anoth surface on which to reinforce brand messages. In their own right they can be so appealin that some people collect the Cole Henley made his collecti into a coffee table.

Campervan's normal open, friendly, simple style is suspended for their barley wine. The bottle shape, simple design and spot varnish finish on the logo all suggest this is a super-premium product that sits apart on its own.

MEANTIME

When Alastair Hook launched Meantime in London in 1999, he wanted to do something no other brewery was yet doing. He adored cask ale, but was frustrated that beer drinkers divided into those who ignored it and thought it was old-fashioned, or those who loved it and viewed every other beer as inferior. Hook – who trained as a brewer in Germany – wanted to revive and rehabilitate forgotten or maligned beer styles wherever they were from. Now we'd call this a craft brewer, but the term didn't exist in the UK at the time.

While Meantime excelled in creating authentic versions of German lager styles, Hook knew he had two great, much-maligned beer styles sitting on his doorstep: IPA and porter were both born in London, and Hook wanted to bring them back in their authentic forms.

Both beers were high in alcohol by modern standards, and didn't suit consumption by the pint. So Meantime launched them in 750ml bottles, clearly positioned for sharing, and presented with food matches. This was beer presented as wine, with the cork and wire finish closing the deal.

Such beers may be more common today, but in the early 2000s Meantime broke the mould and helped people see beer in a different light.

THE ORKNEY BREWERY

Orkney Brewery's Dark Island ale is rich and chocolatey, and has twice been named Champion beer of Scotland. To create Dark Island Reserve, quantities of the beer are aged in Orkney malt whisky casks for three months, giving it a whole new character and a massive boost in ABV to 10%.

When the beer was launched, Orkney wanted to create a super-premium, unique and special beer that set new standards in Britain in the quality of both the product and its packaging.

Each bottle is hand crafted and labelled with the individual Gyle number. The amount produced is deliberately limited so that every bottle can be hand-signed by Andrew Fulton, Orkney's head brewer. The flip-top closure allows resealing of a beer you many not want to finish in one evening, and the paper seal over the flip-top reassures you that no one else has had a quick nip from the bottle before you obtained it.

The bottle cap may be small but it's still a surface that can be used to communicate an extra branding message. Many brands simply repeat the brand name or logo. St Stefanus carries an image inspired by the stained glass in the abbey where the beer was originally brewed: an extra little aesthetic gift to the drinker, as well as a reminder of the brand's authenticity.

Sometimes effective branding is simple and obvious. Small Beer devotes itself exclusively to brewing beers that sit between 1% and just over 2% ABV. The bottle shape stands out from the pack at the same time as reinforcing the brand message.

Belgian beer bottles have such a distinctive shape that when Donzoko wanted to brew a Belgian-style saison, all they had to do to communicate information about the beer style was package it in this distinctive 375ml bottle with a cork and wire closure instead of the cans they normally use.

Old Tom is a strong barley wine-style beer that was first brewed by Robinsons in 1899. While it is redesigned from time to time, like all long-standing beers are, what's consistent is a Victorian-style bottle with unique embossing that sets the brand apart from standard beer ranges.

ST PETER'S

John Murphy already knew a thing or two about designing effective branding when he decided to start a brewery: as founder and chair of consultancy Interbrand he was responsible for the naming of brands including McVitie's Hobnobs, the Ford Mondeo and Viagra. When Murphy retired in 1996, he bought St Peter's Hall in Suffolk and started a real ale brewery with the specific intention of creating beers for export. He knew he wanted the brand to be distinctive, and felt that it should convey ideas of traditional quality and craft.

The design of the 500ml bottle does all that on its own. It's based on a bottle Murphy discovered at an antiques fair, and is believed to be a gin bottle dating from around 1770, manufactured for Thomas Gerrard, an innkeeper in Philadelphia. Its distinctive oval shape immediately stands out. It looks old-fashioned, yet has been gently updated to look contemporary too. It immediately suggests a brand with a story and has been key to making St Peter's an international success.

GROLSCH

Grolsch is arguably unique in having built its brand in the UK – most probably by accident – on the back of its flip-top bottle closure.

Grolsch is a Dutch beer that was launched into the UK in 1984, and subsequently rode the premium bottled lager wave thanks to its distinctive closure. It educated drinkers on how to open and close the bottle, and was seen as something different and something of higher quality: the swing-top is chunky and consists of various parts, and is clearly more expensive to produce than a standard crown cap.

But Groslch's fame was cemented when boy band Bros began wearing Grolsch bottle-tops on their shoes at the height of their fame. Their metal arms were threaded through shoelace eyelets and worn as fake buckles, making a peculiar clinking sound as people walked. This became a national trend – problematically, in schools – among young Bros fans.

When Grolsch was withdrawn from sale in the UK after years of decline, the loss of the bottle-tops was mourned more than the beer.

Fans will be delighted to learn that the brand was relaunched in the UK – bottle-top intact – in 2020.

the mid-2000s, craft beer took off in Italy, a country more famed for its wine than beer. young craft brewers used wine ottles out of necessity rather than choice, but the result was beers that screamed quality and desirability. It's worked so ell that British brewers such as London Beer Factory have appropriated it for their premium beers.

Cans, growlers and crowlers

By their nature, cans have less variation than bottles. Where cans are concerned, the innovation is the can itself, and the fact that it is now considered a premium format. Until recently, despite the protestations of brewers, people believed that cans tainted the flavour of beer. Brewers insist they do not: aluminium cans are lined with a polymer that should prevent any flavour taint, and cans keep the beer fresher than bottles do. There is an argument that it's all psychological, that we expect it to taste metallic. Another theory is that when people drink straight from the can, you're tasting the can itself as it touches your bottom lip, not the beer. The growth of craft beer in cans suggests there's merit in both arguments: psychologically, cans have suddenly become a premium format, and craft beer drinkers are much more likely to pour the beer into a glass rather than drinking it straight from the can.

Cans and bottles are evolving as craft beer shakes up the beer market. Growlers, which first emerged in America in 1989, are a smart evolution from when people used to take their own bottles or even a bucket to take beer home from the pub. Ideal for brewpubs and taprooms that are not big enough to invest in a bottling or canning machine, the growler is a refillable vessel that contains three or four pints of beer. Crowlers take the same principle into canning. Oskar Blues – the pioneers of craft beer cans in 2002 – later acquired a bar-top canning machine that allows cans to be filled from draught line for take-home sales.

Massive can or mini-keg?
Either way, this large container
gives brands like Whitstable Bay a
much bigger CAN-vas (sorry, Ed)
on which to express their design.

's a simple but effective move: aluminium cans are silver. Make yours black,
nd you've changed the canvas compared to most other craft beers.

As larger, returnable and refillable containers that are not brand specific, growlers provide an interesting alternative canvas on which to do overall brewery branding. Barnsley's Nailmaker (below) goes in a different direction, with disposable plastic pouches for volume sales.

'because you're worth it'

8

Beyond the Label

SINCE

T

JAIPUR

JAIPUR

INDIA PALE ALE

Over the top

Beer design doesn't end with the package the beer comes in. The fact that we often tend to want to buy more than one beer at a time necessitates secondary packaging that provides yet more opportunities to stand out.

Even the multiples we buy beer in says something about the beer itself. The 20- or 24-can 'slab' of mainstream lager we buy in supermarkets suggests value to the purchaser, but its bulk nature suggests commodification and low quality to its critics. It's telling that craft beer multi-packs tend to be smaller. This works at a smaller level too: mainstream lager favours the six-pack, whereas premium ales and craft beers tend to go for four-packs.

The multipack is usually a cardboard box or liner that provides a huge canvas for a creative brand, or if you're a mainstream lager, an absolutely massive logo that should be big enough for any brand manager. Designers refer to this as 'billboarding': creating a big, solid block of branding on-shelf.

Six-packs and four-packs are most commonly associated with plastic rings that allow them to be carried in one hand. Recently these have come under fire thanks to their tendency to turn up in marine litter, particularly when strangling wildlife, so forward-thinking brewers are seeking alternatives. In 2018 Carlsberg introduced a new kind of glue that holds cans together. Other brewers are creating edible or biodegradable six-pack rings. But the growing trend among craft brewers is to invest in highly finished overboxes for cans. This is an expensive investment that isn't necessary for practical reasons. But in an ever-more crowded market, it helps achieve that billboarding effect and creates greater standout. It also guarantees that our branding remains front and centre at all times, whereas cans can be spun around on-shelf so the primary branding is obscured.

But secondary packaging is not just limited to multipacks: it can have a great impact for individual bottles too. Nothing says special like putting a beer bottle in its own individual box. It doesn't need one, it's already in a clearly branded bottle, but the extra expense immediately screams 'collector's item', and transforms a bottle of beer into a thoughtful gift.

Orbit's use of a simple wooden case pulls off the neat trick of looking authentic, craft and anti-marketing, at the same time as being highly distinctive and suggesting premiumness.

BREWDOG

BrewDog, at the height of their confrontational period, took secondary packaging to its ultimate conclusion. In 2010 End of History caused a sensation by reclaiming the honour of being the world's strongest beer, at 55%. The name came from the title of Frances Fukuyama's book claiming that Western liberal democracy had reached its evolutionary end-point, and was borrowed by BrewDog to say that this would be the 'final episode' in their quest to produce ever-stronger beers.

Only eleven bottles were ever released, selling at a mere £500 each. The packaging was created by taxidermist Tony Armitstead and all the animals used were roadkill, comprising seven stoats and four grey squirrels. Each one came with its own certificate of authenticity.

'The impact of The End of History is a perfect conceptual marriage between art, taxidermy and craft brewing,' said BrewDog at the time. The bottles are at once beautiful and disturbing – they disrupt conventions and break taboos, just like the beer they hold within them.'

CARLSBERG

Green in every way

Thanks to a long-running dispute between the brewery founder and his son, Carlsberg is today majority-owned by a philanthropic foundation that has a legal obligation to invest in scientific and social initiatives. This has seen the brewery invest millions in sustainability over the last few years to try to reduce its impact on the environment. By 2030 it aims to have zero carbon footprint and a 50% reduction in its water usage, hoping eventually to eliminate waste water altogether. Many of its initiatives are genuinely innovative, and together they point the way towards a possible future for beer packaging.

Packaging accounts for 40% of all Carlsberg's carbon footprint – double that of any other stage of the production or distribution process. In particular, the plastic six-pack rings that hold beer cans together have become emblematic of the harm human rubbish causes to marine and bird life.

In 2018, the brewery launched a whole raft of green packaging initiatives, including:

- The 'Snap Pack', which replaced plastic shrink wrap or plastic rings on multipacks with an innovative glue solution, reducing plastic usage by up to 76%.

- Green ink is, ironically, one of the least environmentally friendly colours to make. So Carlsberg have spent a great deal of time and money working with scientists to develop a new 'greener' green for their packaging.

- New shrink film that contains 50–100% recycled plastic.

- 100% recycled plastic in some plastic bottles, and a reduction in weight of other bottles, saving 550 tonnes of virgin plastic material.

- In 2019, Carlsberg then introduced a 'green fibre bottle' that was essentially a usable beer bottle made from fully recyclable paper. It was hailed instantly as a design triumph.

The clever part is that all this was done at the same time as a major brand redesign. There's a resistance to sustainability initiatives on the grounds that they can cheapen the look and feel of products. Carlsberg refreshed its visual identity at the same time as working with new inks and materials, meaning the newer, more sustainable packaging actually looks better than the old stuff.

The Pursuit of Better Beer

Fuller's first launched Vintage Ale in 1997. Since then it's been an annual release that aims to showcase the best malts and hops used by the brewery that year. The beer matures and develops in the bottle, so different vintages can be collected and compared. This elegant box reinforces its value as a gift.

Here's a neat trick that makes Purity's gift pack work far harder than it should: thanks to a bit of clever thinking, the beer glass handle becomes the handle for the gift pack itself.

Generation Ale was launched in 2011 to commemorate five generations of Shepherd Neame as an independent family brewery. Only 3,000 bottles were released, in bottles that were wrapped in paper then packaged in a wooden presentation box.

paper wrap is a simple way of adding quality. It also some does of the ork the bottle label usually does, allowing designers to do something ore minimalist on the bottle itself.

Overboxes provide a great opportunity to display a brand at scale, giving design room to breathe.
Used creatively, they can also be varied to create a striking collage effect.

'the king of beers'

The Beer Design Hall of Fame

Great beer design is the summation of many different elements and skills. So what do the specialists in each area make of our selection of designs?

We selected six beers featured in this book because in one way or another, they are notable for their striking design. We presented them to a panel of design industry experts: a commercial design strategist, a graphic designer, an illustrator and a typographer, and asked them what they thought.

We gave no background or context – who these brands were, what they were trying to do, or whether we thought they were good or bad – and asked them to judge the design work for itself, on its own merits. One of our panel members was steeped in the world of beer design, the other three knew little or nothing about the beer world, and were seeing most of these designs for the very first time.

A matter of taste

Malcolm Garrett – who began his own design career creating record sleeves for bands such as Buzzcocks – looks here at the clash between sober respectability and punky energy in beer design.

'The packaging of alcoholic drinks like wine and beer seems to be forever looking to find some balance between heritage and frivolous excitement.

'A traditional, sober typographic format implies reliability borne of years of refinement. It reflects a drink whose quality can be trusted and apparently enjoyed for generations. This is most evident in the marketing of wine, and especially in mature spirits such as single malt whisky, where the age is a genuine component of the taste and not simply of the presentation.

'Beer on the other hand, is a product with a shorter shelf life where the obvious disposability of the package encourages consumption over consideration of the contents. The need to stand out from the competition, on the super-market shelf or behind the bar, encourages an approach to packaging that challenges all notions of how to represent taste or quality, and replaces it with a wild mix of vibrant graphic styles, far from sober and seemingly drunk with excitement.

'Designs on beer cans seem to have abandoned any attempt to represent the actual liquid within, and instead appeal directly to the drinker's state of mind. Intended for a youthful audience, brought up on computer games and living in a trainer-collecting culture, it appears that the youth-oriented "alcopops" of the early 90s have grown up to become rebellious teenagers, with all their dubious charm.

'It's perhaps unfair to single out any brand for detailed comment, but if you consider the raw, jagged patterns of Magic Rock alongside the simple, bold typography of Camden Brewery it's already making it feel like a relatively staid veteran.

'Quite simply it comes down to a battle between authority and credibility, whether it's Guinness (est. 1759) or Partizan (est. 2012). Both are trying hard: the evolution of the Guinness harp logo trying hard to look contemporary, without abandoning any of its implicit references to quality and traditional flavour, and Partizan, well, just trying too hard.

'Somewhere in between is Kernel, with a graphic language that's both youthful and traditional. A plain brown paper label and "vintage" brown bottle suggests an "honesty" that contemporary competitors have wilfully abandoned.

'Given the reliance on visual prominence to distinguish itself in a crowded market it is quite natural that packaging of beer has become increasingly outrageous, but I'll always remember Worthington's "it's the taste that satisfies".'

The panel

Silas Amos, *commercial designer*:
A designer and design strategist, Silas has spent over thirty years working with beer brands such as Boddingtons, Stella Artois, Budweiser and Guinness. It's involved helicopters to Monte Carlo, patting Budweiser Clydesdales noses in St Louis, and getting hands-on training on pulling a proper pint of Guinness from the head brewer. 'The best job in the world is working with breweries,' he says. 'There's just a bit more soul and poetry in branding a beer than there is doing an identity for a bank.'   silasamos.com

Malcolm Garrett MBE RDI, *graphic design guru*: Malcolm Garrett is Creative Director of the design consultancy Images&Co, with offices in London and Manchester. He is a Founder and Artistic Director of the annual Design Manchester festival. With a collaborative, multi-disciplinary and user-focused approach to design, Malcolm's career spans four decades. At art school in Manchester in 1977 he founded the graphic design group Assorted iMaGes, and later in 1994 the pioneering digital agency AMX. Working at the interface of digital, virtual and real-world experience, he has gone on to lead numerous design projects, both local and international, for artists, businesses large and small, community groups and in the public sector. malcolmgarrett.com, images.co.uk
Twitter: @malcolmgarrett
Instagram: @beingmalcolmgarrett

Neil Gower, *illustrator*: Neil is an award-winning graphic artist best known for his illustrated maps and book jacket designs, most notably for William Golding and Bill Bryson. (And perhaps less notably, but no less loved, for some of this author's books, including *Hops & Glory*, *Man Walks into a Pub*, and Miracle Brew.)   neilgower.com

Sarah Hyndman, *typographer*: Sarah is the author of books including the best-selling *Why Fonts Matter*, and is the founder of 'Type Tasting'. She's a TEDx speaker, a regular on radio and occasionally pops up on TV. As a multisensory typography expert, she's co-published studies with Professor Charles Spence of the University of Oxford. Not much of a beer drinker, she nevertheless feels that 'My 20-something-year-old self would have been very happy swigging from a can of Vocation along with my John Player Special black cigarettes, DMs and leather jacket!'   typetasting.com

Guinness

SA: 'Guinness continue to achieve the remarkable trick of feeling contemporary and "cult" after hundreds of years of brewing, and decades in basically the same livery. They appear unspoilt by progress. The new highly crafted harp offers a "maximalist" design in a category populated by simpler, more minimalist designs. Maximalist design isn't easy – and the visual craft suggests equal attention to detail in the brewing process. When I was working on this brand it commissioned a global semiotic review that suggested the harp was a feminine instrument and thus we might consider dropping it. This confirmed all my prejudices about the redundancy of academic semiotics. Happily, it was also perceived as an instrument that is "hard to make and hard to play", which resonates with a beer that goes the extra mile.'

Lost & Grounded

SA: 'The overall impression is of an explosion in a Hoxton illustration agency. One can be cynical about this – what's hot right now isn't necessarily going to remain timeless like a Guinness or even Camden. That is to miss the point: this isn't design created for longevity; it's to celebrate the *now*. It's for beer magpies, and when we look back in twenty years it will represent a wonderful time capsule of the design of our times, much as LP covers represent the various strata of hip design back down the years. Drink three of your cans, and put one on the shelf – one day there will be a lively eBay trade in these mini time capsules of "hot right now" design. That's fun. And the joy of such design is a very happy drinking partner to the joy of appreciating good beer.'

SH: 'This feels more like a daytime, festival beer. It's telling you that it's wholesome – it's made in nature, or from natural ingredients, and that drinking it is like taking a breath of fresh air.'

Camden

SA: 'A more huggable version of BrewDog, Camden have done a smashing job of bottling their natural enthusiasm and character. They look cool without feeling try-hard, and have built a "design system" across their range that works without feeling cookie-cutter. The key to their success is partly about working with great design and illustration talent. Partnering with current and cool talent is one of their passions, and it's paid off very well. The impression they give is that they are very focused on "properly brewed" beer that satisfies the nerds, but that they wear this lightly. The colours are fantastic – there is something intangibly yet quintessentially "Camden, London" that just hits the spot. And they do it in a way that is distinctive enough that they won't be easy to carbon copy.'

SH: 'I like the typographic approach (of course!). The labels make me think of Victorian display type on letterpress posters for music halls and carnivals, but with a contemporary feel. I think this suggests the craft of the printing process combined with tradition or traditional recipes going back a century or so – but it's refreshed for today's aesthetic and palate.'

The Kernel

SA: 'Kernel is the visual equivalent of a humble brag: "We are so confident of our beer and so focused on its quality that we have no time for the superfluous business of glossy labelling", it says. It stands as an example of peak "authentic hipster craft" design, a badge for drinkers keen to let you know they are keeping it real.'

SH: 'The DIY and minimalist printed black type on brown wrapping paper feels homemade. These are signifiers of small batch/craft production that can be seen across so many products, including those craft kettle chips you're likely to be eating with your beer. The apparently understated appearance tells you the beer is important, not the design. It feels nonchalant, but as a graphic designer I know that a great deal of consideration goes into making a design look effortless.'

Mikkeller

NG: 'The Mikkeller designs recall the wine labels for Chateau Mouton Rothschild, which has been commissioning from artists such as Mirò, Picasso, Francis Bacon and Jeff Koons since 1945. This makes each design feel like an event in itself. It strikes me now that these wine labels are a means of harnessing both the heritage of a name and fresh, constantly reinvented visuals – a combination that the designers of these beers brands have been conspicuously aware of.'

SH: 'These designs are more modern, not referencing craftsmanship or brewing history. It feels to me like they're telling you about the intended audience, not the provenance of the beer. They make me think of DIY zines, comic books and sticker collections with illustrations created using computers and collage. I'm guessing the designs keep changing so each batch of beer feels unique?'

Vocation

SH: 'This makes me think of classic tattoos, seaside towns at night and lettering artists. Cheeky, edgy and cool. It suggests the skill of the craftsperson and the fun of a night out with your friends thinking you're being cool. The black background gives it an edgy, night-time with neon lights and leather biker jackets atmosphere.'

NG: 'While some of this imagery is naive in execution, there is a punchy sophistication to the overall aesthetic.'

Partizan

SH: 'I think this suggests the traditional artistry of making beer. The illustrations remind me of the Dubonnet poster by A.M. Cassandre, so it's about classic artistry in a modern world. The illustrations have layers of storytelling so you can decode the meanings and feel clever whilst savouring your beer.'

NG: 'It is interesting and encouraging to note the increased use of illustrative content. This is a wilful move away from the "traditional" approach that once characterised beer aesthetics. While one has to question the potential longevity of these designs, they feel fabulously nimble, and are unquestionably seductive. They echo the creativity of the new generation of brewers. Established brands must be finding it very difficult to compete, with their feet tied by their own design heritage.'

Image credits

Thanks to all the featured breweries who provided images:

Adnams (Cookchick Design); Allendale; Almasty (Andrew Linaker); Amity (Tom Matthews); Ampersand (Craig Cutting); And Union; Anspach & Hobday (Alan Batley); Atom (Gavin Appleby Design); Badger (BrandOpus); Barney's Beer (photographer Roberto Ricciuti); Beavertown (Nick Dwyer); Beck's; BeerbleFish (Bethany Burrow, Atherton, Thunderclap Creative, Sara Bailey); Black Iris (Kev Grey); Boundary (John Robinson, Phil Harrison); Brew By Numbers (Pentagram); Brew York (United by Design); BrewDog (Tony Armitstead (taxidermist); Brick Brewery (Twin pixels CGI, More than Equal, Tor Ewen); Brixton Brewery (Junction Studio); Budvar (We Are Halo); Bullhouse (Thomas Bannon, Shane Walsh); Burning Sky (Simon Gane); Burnt Mill (Josh Smith, Sean Stone); Camden (Studio Juice); Campervan (Nicci Peat); Canopy (People Like Us, illustrators ZEBU, Natalya Balnova, Camilla Perkins, Oh Papa, Aysha Tengiz, Aga Giecko, Bo Matteini); Caps Off (Brent); Carlsberg (Taxi Studio); Chiltern; Cloak & Dagger (Leigh Pearce, We Are Lolly); Cloudwater (Textbook Studio); Coast (James Ockelford, Refold Design); Cromarty (Ben Edwards); Crooked Brewing (Neil Hogan, Orangepeel); Deya (Thom Hobson); Donzoko (Sean Edgar); Double-Barrelled (Kingdom & Sparrow); Drygate (Rob Mackay); Duration (Joe Conway, James Beeson, Mark Newton, 5HT Design); Dynamite Valley (Kingdom & Sparrow); Edinburgh Beer Factory (Jones Knowles Ritchie); Exale (Adam Brazier); Firebrand (Kingdom & Sparrow); Five Points (Kate Lyons); Fourpure (Peter Saville); Framework (Lee Garton and Mat Mabe at Bulb Studios); Fuller's; Full Circle (O Street); Gipsy Hill (Marcus Reed); Good Chemistry (Confederation Studio); Guinness (Design Bridge); Hackney Brewery (Pete Fowler, Colophon Foundry); Harvey's (WPA Pinfold); Heineken; Howling Hops (Thumbcrumble, Pete Holt, Lewis Heriz); Hydes (WPA Pinfold); Innis & Gunn (Diarmid Scott, Carlo Paloni); Iron Pier (Duncan Grant); JW Lees (Squad); Kernel (Ute Kanngiesser); Leigh on Sea Brewery (Neil Fendell, Nick Pettit); Lincoln Green (Nick Law @Hop Forward Designs); Loch Ness (Thirst Craft); London Beer Factory (James Leaver); London Fields (Luke McLean); Lost & Grounded (Sam Davis, Alexia Tucker); Magic Rock (Rich Norgate); Magic Spells (James Mayall); Marble (Jan Barker); Maule (England Diep); Meantime; Mikkeller (Keith Shore); Moor Beer Company (Ich Bin Ben); Moorhouses (WPA Pinfold); Mondo (Luke Drozd); Mothership (Jane Frances LeBlond); Mourne Mountains (Gareth McGivern, Olivia Catherine Rooney, Ian Sands); Neptune (John McKeown, Eyes Wide Design); New Bristol (Tom Moore); Newbarns (Jonah Schulz); No Heroes (Russell Miller); North (James Ockelford, Refold Design) Northern Monk (Mark Newton, Jon Simmon, James Butler); Orbit (ByVolume); Overtone (Thirst Craft); Partizan (Alec Doherty); Peroni/Asahi; Pilot (Matt Johnson/Patrick Jones @Pilot); Pomona Island (Martin Halliwell, Meiko Kimura-Bee); Pressure Drop (Sienna O'Rourke, Ching-Li Chew); Purity (Zunaira Muzafar, Beth Nicol); Red Willow (Big Brand Ideas, Emily Taylor); Robinsons; Roosters; Round Corner; Sambrooks (Firuzé French); Seven Brothers (Creative Spark); Shepherd Neame; Signature Brew (B&B Studio); Siren (Studio Parr); six°north (Matt Carrington); Small Beer (Kingdom & Sparrow); Solvay Society (Harry Archer, Sarah Sinclair); Squawk Brewing Company (Camille Smithwick, designs by KnownAim Graphic and Design Studio); Staggeringly Good; (Hannah Horn); Tapestry (Gavin Andrews, Thirty Three + Rebel); Thornbridge (Thirst Craft); Thwaites (WPA Pinfold); Timothy Taylor's (Springetts Design); Tiny Rebel (Tamsin Baker); To Øl (Kasper Ledet); Turning Point (Lottie Walsh); Unity Brewing (Matt Canning); Untapped (Jordan Mower); Verdant (Cornish Creatives); Vocation (Robot Food); Wander Beyond (Tina Breslin); Weird Beard (Chris Walker @Doodlebank); Whiplash (Sophie Devere); Whitby; Whitstable Bay (Shepherd Neame); Wild Card (Howard Cope, Valero Doval); Wild Beer Co (Miller Design); Williams Bros (Mil Stricevic); Wiper and True (Studio Mackgill); Wylam (Sally Lindsay at Real Eyes); Young's (Kingdom & Sparrow). *Also*: Tom Morley; Nottingham Craft Beer Week; Cole Henley; Jones Knowles Ritchie; Beer Merchants (for Belgian beer images).

Index of brands

CAMRA Books

Modern British Beer
MATTHEW CURTIS

This book is about why modern British beer is important. Over the course of the past two decades the British beer scene as we know it has changed, forever. Matthew Curtis gives a personal insight into the eclectic and exciting world of modern British beer from a choice of 86 influential brews; from how they taste, how their ingredients are sourced, to the engaging stories of the people behind the scenes working hard to bring exciting beer to drinkers all over Britain. This book is a fantastic starting point to explore British beer with an exciting location closer than you think.

RRP **£15.99**   ISBN 978-1-85249-370-

A Year in Beer
JONNY GARRETT

Chefs have been telling us to eat seasonally for decades, yet, when it comes to drink, we tend to reach for the same thing, whatever time o year. But beer is inextricably linked to the seasons, and thinking abou it all seasonally opens the door to even greater beer experiences. *A Year in Beer* is an exploration of how our ingredients and tastes change with the seasons, and how Britain's rich brewing history still influences us today. Discover the best UK beer experiences, from summer beer festivals to the autumn hop and apple harvests — taking in the glory of the seasons that make them all possible.

RRP **£15.99**   ISBN 978-1-85249-372

World Beer Guide
ROGER PROTZ

The world of beer is on fire. Traditional brewing countries are witnessing a spectacular growth in the number of beer makers while drinkers in such unlikely nations as France and Italy are moving from the grape to the grain. Drawing on decades of experience, Roger Protz takes readers on a journey of discovery around the world's favourite alcoholic drink — uncovering the interlinked stories behind the best breweries and beers across every continent in the world.

RRP **£30** (Hardback)   ISBN 978-1-85249-373-

Order these and other CAMRA Books from **shop.camra.org.u**